There's a Pig
on the
Playground

There's a Pig on the Playground

Memorable Stories from the Schoolyard

Deanna Gilmore, Ph.D.

Published by Schoolyard Press

ISBN(paperback): 979-8-9988974-0-5
ISBN (ebook): 979-8-9988974-1-2

Book design and production by www.AuthorSuccess.com

Printed in the United States of America

To my late husband, Rick Gilmore who always encouraged me to be all that I can be.

Contents

Foreword

"There's no better way to start a day than with bacon, but it's much better when you don't have to wrangle it yourself."

This is the lesson from Tony Bonuccelli's story in *There's a Pig on the Playground*, Deanna Gilmore's engaging memoir about her life and the educators, administrators, bus drivers, cafeteria staff, aides, and others who shaped our early experiences.

Attending school—whether at home at a multi-grade schoolhouse in a prairie town, a Native Alaskan village, or an all-girls Catholic school in the city—is a universal experience. For many, it is the first time we spend hours under the care and instruction of adults who are not our parents. We learn significant subjects such as English, history, math, and science. However, we also gain insights about ourselves and the world around us.

This book is part memoir and part collaboration. Deanna Gilmore offers a glimpse into her early days, sitting on her father's lap while he operates the combine on their farm in Plaza, Washington, a town with an unchanged population of fifty-six. She recalls the "snow patterns" on her family's first television set, meeting and falling in love with her husband, Rick, and the challenges of giving birth in a remote village in Alaska. Her personal joys and tribulations become ours through her narrative.

Deanna's book transported me not only to Eastern Washington and remote Alaskan villages I have never visited but also back to Sharon Center, Ohio, in the 1980s. I envisioned Mrs. Horsey, my second-grade teacher of similar height, who helped zip up my coat every day before recess. I remembered Mrs. Sexhauer, the music teacher who taught us minstrel hits like "Jimmy Crack Corn," using these songs to educate us about slavery. My sixth grade English teacher, Mary McNeil, corrected us whenever we called her "Mrs." instead of "Ms.," imparting my first lesson in feminism. Our bus driver, Mrs. Bambeck, drilled us on how to safely exit the yellow school bus from the back.

Today's teachers, administrators, maintenance and office staff, bus drivers, food service workers, and coaches face even greater challenges than those of previous generations. Schools have never been merely places to learn academic subjects; they are environments where children should be safe, have access to healthy meals, discover new interests, develop friendships, and learn about life.

It is fitting that Deanna's memoir includes contributions from others who played a role in raising generations of our nation's children. This collaborative approach aligns with her life's work and dedication.

While we may never know the truth about Deanna's 'freckle juice' and whether it caused her student's emergency appendectomy, we do recognize that Deanna, her husband, and the millions of professionals who dedicate their lives to educating our children are the unsung heroes of our nation.

"The more we get together, the happier we'll be." Enjoy this read.

Lynn Tramonte is co-author of *Broken Hope: Deportation and the Road Home* and editor of the *Ohio Migration Anthology* series.

Introduction

What would you do if this happened to you? You are teaching twenty-five third-grade students and it is time for morning recess. They are in a straight line waiting to rush onto the playground. You look out the window and see a fat little pink pig running around. If you let the students outside, utter chaos will ensue and there may be no way to contain the situation.

Well, that is what is happening in our schools today. We have a crisis on our hands. Since the COVID-19 pandemic, teachers have been leaving the teaching profession in droves. They cite lower pay compared to other professions, increased responsibilities because of the lack of teachers, and at times they fear for their lives. In 2024, there were an estimated 400,000 unfilled teaching positions in all the states, or the positions were filled by uncertified teachers. In many districts, there were not enough bus drivers to get our children to school.

I know this because I spent over forty years in the field of education. First as an elementary teacher, Title I reading teacher, and teaching Alaskan Natives for eight years in remote Eskimo villages. Then, I became an elementary school principal in Montana four years. I taught special education students in Ireland, and upon my return to the United

States, I obtained a Ph.D. in literacy from Washington State University at the age of sixty. Finally, I spent my last seventeen years in education as an assistant professor of preservice teachers at Washington State University and the University of Idaho, where I received the Alumni Award for Excellence in Teaching.

With my varied background in education, I thought, what can I do to help this situation? I cannot give people raises, but I can tell my story of how I became a teacher as well as share true stories from other players in the schoolyard. Our true stories might inspire people to get a job in the field of education. After interviewing many people, I realized that in spite of the hard days and long nights, they do their jobs out of love for the students in their care. These are our 'unsung heroes.' I hope you enjoy reading all of our stories.

PART ONE

Elementary Years

CHAPTER ONE

Put Your Hand Down

DEANNA PETERSCHICK, AGE SIX

"Deanna, put your hand down. You have to give the other children a chance to answer."

That was my first cousin talking, who also happened to be my first-grade teacher. Was this a blessing or a curse that she would be my teacher at Plaza Grade School? There were only four students in my class, and I had the notion that I might be the teacher's pet because she was the daughter of my favorite aunt, Rose Churchill. It didn't look like that was going to happen.

My cousin Dorothy was very pretty with wavy dark hair and she had a dimple on her chin. She looked a lot like Aunt Rose, but I really didn't know her very well. She was twenty-two years older than me, and because of that we didn't play together when we were little.

Our school was a red brick building and it had two large rooms in it. One room was for students in grades one to four and it was called, the 'little room.' Across the highly polished wooden floor was the 'big room,' where classes were held for grades five through eight. Dorothy's husband Roger taught the older students in the 'big room.'

My teacher grew up in Plaza, Washington, on my aunt and uncle's wheat and pea farm, so it was natural for her to return home to get her first teaching job at Plaza Grade School. Like Dorothy's parents, most of the people in Plaza were farmers whose grandparents had homesteaded or purchased the rich, fertile ground that surrounded the town. This land was called the Palouse country, where many people called it the 'breadbasket of the world.' It probably was, in our small view.

As you drove through Plaza, you saw a white metal sign with black letters alongside the highway and it said, "Plaza, population 56."

I asked my dad, "How come the population of Plaza never changes?"

Without missing a lick, he said, "Because every time a new baby is born, someone leaves town."

The only store in Plaza was located right on the highway that passed through it. If you stepped a foot off the gravel in front of the store, you might get hit by a car passing through town. The store was called Murphy's, named after the owner, and it was also the local post office. It had four tall wooden white poles on the porch and it looked like you could hitch a horse to them.

Since it was also the post office, my parents would drive to town to get their mail, and they used a brass key to retrieve it from the cubicles on the wall.

Murphy's had a long oak counter, and on the left hand side was a huge gold cash register, or at least I thought it was gold. It had leaves and vines etched on each side, and every time someone purchased goods, the drawer flew open with a loud 'ding!' To the right of the cash register was a round glass-covered case that housed the penny candy and Hershey bars. I guess the glass was meant to deter any nimble fingers from grabbing the Double Bubble gum inside.

We lived about a mile from Murphy's store, and when I got older I would walk there with a gunny sack in hand. Along the way, I found glass beer or pop bottles in the ditch and filled my sack. I gave it to Mr. Murphy and I got a penny for each bottle I collected. Then, I would carefully select some penny candy from the shelves below. It was mostly Double Bubble gum and orange marshmallow peanuts. If I had a big haul that day, I bought a whole Hershey bar or Milky Way for ten cents.

Every small farm town in Eastern Washington had a tavern, and Plaza's was directly across the highway from Murphy's store. It was a narrow light green wooden building and looked like a boxcar from a train. I used to go in there and sit on the high red plastic stools at the bar, where I spun around and around waiting for my dad to finish his beer. My dad usually bought me a tall bottle of Nesbit orange soda, and that made the wait a little easier.

As it happened, many of the farmers in the area were of German descent, having emigrated to the US from Germany. My grandparents were Emil and Lena Peterschick. Lena Franz had come to America on a ship when she was only four years old with her parents and little brother. She told me that she and her little brother were seasick all the way over and that the captain of the ship told her mother that if they didn't quit throwing up and getting sick, he would throw them overboard. That obviously didn't happen because she ended up in the Palouse country and married my grandpa, Emil. Emil had come out

West from Wisconsin with his brother Frank to purchase farmland in Plaza.

Most of our neighbors were also German. I was born in 1942 during the war, so I was well aware of my heritage. When I grew up, I used to watch movies at the small theatre in Rosalia, Washington, and I remember seeing black and white newsreels with Hitler and his soldiers marching through the streets of Germany. It really scared me, and I also realized that many people in our area did not like Germans. I could never really understand why people talked so badly about the Germans when my grandparents were so nice and kind. I know that my father spoke German until he went to school, but he abruptly quit speaking it because of the association with the war.

My grandmother, Lena, was a short woman with light blonde hair always pulled back in a bun. She wore high-top shoes with heels that clicked every time she walked across the linoleum floors in the kitchen. She was known in Plaza for making the best homemade German noodles. I watched her while she rolled out the dough, put it around a rolling pin, pulled out the pin, then started cutting the noodles. She was known to have the thinnest noodles in the country, and she cut them so fast I could barely catch up with her. She boiled them, then browned butter in a pan and poured it over the cooked noodles. She added salt and pepper, and then my cousin Judy and I would scarf them down like candy.

Grandpa Emil was a rotund man who wore striped overalls and always had a mischievous grin. He would sit in his wicker rocking chair in the living room and tell stories to us adoring children. If we were good listeners, he would slip us a few pieces of hard candy when Grandma wasn't looking.

One time, we visited Grandpa and Grandma at their small white house on a hill in Plaza, and Grandpa was sitting outside in front of the garage on the driveway. He was sitting on an apple crate because it was handy, rather than pulling a chair out from the kitchen. Right in the middle of a story he was telling us, we heard something go CRACK! Sure enough, Grandpa, who had a little bit of weight on him, broke through the crate. When he stood up to shake it off, it was stuck to his bottom, and we all started howling with laughter. Grandpa joined us because he thought it was funny, too. Grandma was in the kitchen so she didn't get to witness this hilarity. My dad helped pry the crate off Grandpa's backside, and we went on with our day. No one mentioned it to Grandma as we all walked inside the house snickering.

Back to my school and first grade. We lived about a mile south of town, so I couldn't walk to school on my own. I got to ride the big yellow school bus. I stood next to the highway across from our gravel driveway with my metal Cinderella lunchbox in my hand. My mom had packed me a bologna sandwich with bread and mayonnaise and a nice juicy orange. She also packed a small carton of milk inside and sometimes added a chocolate chip cookie. My mom was a good cook, and everyone in Plaza knew it, so sometimes I had to keep the older kids from grabbing my lunchbox and reaching for the cookie inside on the way to school.

I loved riding the bus to school and sitting by Claire Hoff, who was my closest neighbor. She had short blonde hair that curled up on the ends. She was also pretty, so it was easy to have her for my best friend. No more than fifteen children were on the bus on the way to Plaza Grade School. Sometimes, the older boys got rowdy, but our bus driver, a large man in overalls, would yell at them and they would settle down.

My cousin Dorothy, or Mrs. Phillips as we called her, taught me how to read in first grade. She used flashcards and we read *Run, Spot, Run* in the Dick and Jane books. I loved those books and caught on quite easily to learn how to read. I also learned how to count to one hundred and add a few numbers together. I was sad when I had to say goodbye to my teacher on the last day of school. She wasn't so bad after all, but she left after her first year of teaching. She moved to Spokane with her husband.

After a long, hot summer of waiting for school to begin again, I finally got to go on the bus. Now, I was in second grade and had a new teacher named Mrs. Vandenborg. I never knew her first name, because we only used teacher's last names when we grew up. She did not grow up in Plaza but was from the nearby city of Spokane. She always wore dresses past her knees and had a wonderful face and smile. Mrs. Vandenborg was always pleasant and never had to raise her voice to the students. She knew how to control the class by having things for us to do when she wasn't teaching our grade. Since there were four grades in the 'little room,' we always heard what was going on in the other classes and learned from them.

Sometimes we laughed with them. One day, Mrs. Vandenborg had a girl in first grade read a story out loud and she said, "There was a piggy one in the park."

The actual words were, "There was a pigeon in the park," and everyone, including me laughed, not at her, but with her when she realized what she had said.

Besides listening to others' mistakes and good answers, we added two new students to our second-grade class. They were both boys and they were so smart they skipped first grade and came right into our class. I didn't mind because one of the boys had big dimples like, me and he wasn't just smart, but also cute. His name was Denny, and as it happened, his parents and my parents were close friends. Since there were only two boys and three other girls besides me in my class, I called him my boyfriend.

The year went by smoothly and I loved Mrs. Vandenborg so much. On the last day of school, as I was getting on the school bus to go home, I told the bus driver that I had to go in and get something out of my desk before I went home. He patiently opened the bus door with a swish and I jumped down the steps. I entered the classroom, and with tears in my eyes, I ran over to Mrs. Vandenborg and gave her a big hug and whimpered, "Goodbye."

I thought I would never see her again . . . and sure enough, she didn't come back to teach us again.

Another summer rolled by and I got to go with my dad on the combine and watch him harvest the wheat on the hills behind our home. I was a little frightened when he turned on the leveler as we went around the steep parts of the hill. The combine would tilt over just enough to keep going and not tip over as we threshed the wheat in front of us. It would get very hot out there, so I couldn't stay long before I went back into our farmhouse. I was just proud that he let me go with him to see what his job was like on the farm.

CHAPTER 2
Kick the Can

Deanna, Age eight

It was official. I was now old enough to play 'Kick the Can' at Plaza Grade School. There was an unwritten rule that only children in grades three and above could play Kick the Can, and I had reached that age in the summer of 1950. In case you don't know, this is the way you play Kick the Can: Someone might yell out, "You're 'it,' Deanna," in which case I would pick up the empty pop can and set it down in the middle of the gravel playground and yell, "Here I go."

Then, I would cover my eyes and push my little body up against the brick school and start counting from one to fifty, loud enough so everyone could hear. Then all the children would run and hide around the playground, behind the school, under the stairs, and sometimes in the rich soil behind the gravel. I then started looking for my victims one at a time, and if I saw someone, I ran very quickly to the middle of the playground and jumped over the empty tin can yelling, "Over the can on Danny," or whoever the person was.

If someone was very sly, they would wait until I went around one side of the building and run in while I was looking for the other players and kick the can very hard while bursting out, "Kick the can," and we would have to start all over again and I would still be 'it.' This would go on until I finally caught everyone, and the last person I found had to be 'it' the next time around. This continued until the recess bell rang to come inside, and it was glorious!

Third grade was also when I got to join the baseball team. As it was, our school did not have enough students to have our own team, so the girls had to play with the boys just to make one team. Being a girl, I was usually sent to right field, where they hit the fewest balls. I remember looking up at the sun and hoping the ball did not fly in my direction. I did not want to be responsible for losing a game for my team. Sometimes, we actually had teams from nearby towns come on a school bus and play against us. I did my best and I caught a few fly balls to help put away their side. Because of this situation, I was somewhat of a tomboy and could always hold my own in sports.

We also had new teachers who were from the big city of Spokane. They were a married couple and were both very nice. I was now old enough to learn their first names. He was Vern Ronald and she was Verla Ronald. I thought, *just like teachers, to marry people with the same beginning initial.* Mrs. Ronald taught grades one to four and Mr. Ronald taught grades five to eight. They stayed in Plaza for four years, for which we were grateful.

While I was in Mrs. Ronald's room, we had a special visitor from Spokane visit our class. She was dressed like a soldier with a long-sleeved tan shirt tucked in neatly to her straight khaki skirt, and she had a soldier's pointed cap on her head. She was a person from the National Wildlife Service and she came out every year to teach us about Smokey Bear and putting out campfires. I loved it when she came, because she brought a stuffed animal that looked like Smokey Bear and sat him down in front of us while she talked to us about caring for the forest. I always remember that she had a gold tooth and it sparkled when she talked. I don't remember her name, but she impressed me every year she came to speak to us. I was always very mindful of putting out campfires whenever we went camping because of her and Smokey Bear.

Since we had regular teachers who didn't leave us, it was easier to leave school for the summer months. In June, I sat out in the field by our house, watching the cars go by, and ate green peas by the dozens. I was very content to be on the farm and have the sun beat down on my back.

Besides sitting in the field, I often climbed up the roof of our barn. One shingle was missing, and I could see right into the pig pen below. There was one big, fat, mean pig who lived there and I had nightmares about falling through the hole and landing in the mud. Just as the pig was about to charge me, I would wake up and be down at the bottom of the bed.

I also had nightmares about the 'boogeyman' living under the barn, and just as I would reach the last step to go up, he would grab my ankle and pull me down. Again, I woke up before something terrible happened to me. I don't think my parents ever knew how much I worried about falling through that hole because I never told them. It was between me and my dreams.

Another thing I did to occupy my time was to go behind the barn, where there was a big wooden slab my dad used to slaughter the pigs and cut them up for our winter meat and bacon. He washed down the pieces of wood, so in the off-season, I used the wooden slabs as a stage for my future as a movie star. I would put on plays by myself and sometimes I would have my baby brother join in. His name was Jimmy and he had blonde hair combed to one side and a cute little grin. He was only five years old at the time, but he always did as I told him and was a good acting companion. We staged plays with no audience around to judge us.

I did not have too many chores except to feed the chickens and throw out the mash in their chicken coop every day. One day, Jimmy followed me to the chicken coop to feed the chickens. As we were walking back down the path toward our farmhouse, a large white rooster with a yellow beak jumped on my little brother's shoulder and started pecking him on the face. I yelled at the rooster to get off, but he had a strong hold on my brother's neck. I screamed and ran down to the house to get my mom. I told her, "There is a rooster on Jimmy's neck, and I can't get him off."

My mom grabbed a broom from a corner of the kitchen and ran out the door. I followed her and by that time, blood was running down my little brother's neck and I started yelling, "Get him off, Mom."

My mom took two big swings at the rooster's back and it went tumbling to the ground. From that day on, I quit feeding the chickens and left that up to the adults in the family, and I also developed a slight fear of chickens and birds.

That fall, Mom and Dad drove to Spokane and left us with Carolyn so they could buy things they could not get in the neighboring town of Rosalia. Carolyn was six years older than me and she was tall with light, flowing, brown hair. We slept together in an upstairs bedroom in our farmhouse and I looked up to her. One time, we were in bed and she told me that she wrote the song, "On the Boardwalk in Atlantic City." I was thrilled to think that my sister wrote that song and she sang it to me right after telling me that. I later found out she was spoofing me.

It was close to Halloween when Mom and Dad got back from Spokane, and Mom gave me a special treat. She handed me a pink piggy mask made of starched netting and a package of Wrigley's spearmint gum. I was thrilled with my present and looked forward to going trick or treating six miles away in Rosalia. Plaza was too small for trick or treating, and most of the people lived out in the country on their farms. It was too hard to reach them and we wouldn't get much candy. Luckily, the people in Rosalia knew we were coming and were prepared to give the 'Plaza kids' candy.

Halloween finally arrived and we excitedly waited for Dad to come home from doing his chores on the farm. Once he got home when the sun was just beginning to set, we left for Rosalia. Jimmy and I piled into my dad's black Buick and we headed toward the city. It felt like the longest six miles ever that night.

When we got there, my dad parked on the street and Jimmy and I took off running to hit as many houses as we could before it got too cold and dark. We both carried large brown grocery sacks to haul our candy. I stayed warm because I was also wearing a pink fluffy coat to match the pink piggy mask Mom bought me in Spokane.

The people in Rosalia were very generous to us. They handed out oranges and apples, but the best treats were the flat Hershey bars wrapped in their shiny packages and the giant-sized Tootsie Rolls, which were extra special. One of my favorites was the square pieces of Double Bubble gum, and I tried to get as many pieces as the people were willing to hand us.

It started getting dark and I could hear my dad honk his horn, which meant it was all over. We knew we had better run back to the car so he wouldn't get mad at us for taking too long. As I was running down the hill by the high school, I slipped on the icy grass and tumbled down the hill.

My sack broke, but not all the way, and all the candy and fruit flew all over the place. It was pitch black by then and I wasn't going to leave the candy, so I pawed my way through the grass and picked up every piece of candy I could find. I didn't care about the apples and oranges, but I wanted those Tootsie Rolls and Hershey bars I had gathered on that cold night.

The car felt so warm when we got inside and I held on tightly to my sack, hoping nothing would spill out on the way home. When we finally arrived, I grabbed my brown paper bag and dumped it out on the kitchen table ready to see all my loot.

There, in the middle of all the candy, was a large log of dried dog poop. I had mistaken it for a Tootsie Roll that had lost its wrapper. Looking at it with disgust, I had to throw everything away because it was ruined. There went my great day and night of trick or treating and all those Hershey Bars. As I was sobbing, my little brother came over and offered me one of his Hershey bars and some Double Bubble gum. I gladly took it.

Deanna Loses Her Loot!

CHAPTER 3

Marching Rose

That winter, after the Tootsie Roll incident, I went to stay with my Aunt Rose. She was my dad's oldest sister, and since her two daughters were grown and gone from the house, she often borrowed me for the weekends. I think she missed her daughters so she thought she would help raise me. Thank heavens for her wanting.

Rose Peterschick Churchill came from a good hard-working German family and she was a natural born leader. Rose was a pillar of the Plaza community, especially when it came to the Order of Patrons of Husbandry or the Grange. The Grange began in 1867 to help farmers with their economic conditions and to give farmers a social outlet in their communities. There was usually a Grange Hall in every small farming community in the Palouse Country where I grew up. Plaza had its own Grange Hall, and that is where all of our school programs were performed. On some Saturday nights, the Plaza Grange held dances with live bands where we danced the polka, the Schottische, and modern dances like the fox trot and the waltz. Young children could join their parents and I learned how to dance standing on my dad's toes while he twirled me around during the polka.

18

Aunt Rose was very important to the Grange because she played the piano while people marched with the United States flag flying as they took their respective seats. She also led people in singing the opening and leaving songs for the evening. Before the official Grange meeting started, she stood in front of the whole community, raised her arms, and had us follow her in singing something about "the more we get together."

I remember sitting in the front row and gazing up at her with such admiration. I thought that I wanted to be like her and lead people in song. After our initial greeting, the children would be dismissed to the basement of the Grange so the adults could conduct their business. While downstairs, we ran around the basement cement floor and sat on the green painted wooden benches, where we played games. We participated in 'wink um,' where we would sit across from a person of the opposite sex and give them a wink. Whoever we winked at would have to get up and chase us around the basement floor until they caught us. If they didn't catch us before we got back to our original seat, they would be 'it' the next time around. We also played hide and seek, as everyone knew how to play that game.

I had an older cousin who was very handsome for his age of nine, and I remember playing wink um with him and getting the first inkling of what it meant to have a crush on a boy . . . even if it was my cousin.

I could hear the people stomping on the wooden floor above us while they went through their secret ceremonies with my Aunt Rose playing the piano. I could only imagine what they were talking about upstairs, as we were not allowed to join them.

At the end of the official meeting, the adults would climb down the grey stairs to the basement, where they joined us for snacks. We had to have something to eat before we went home. It wouldn't be a Plaza Grange meeting without some food involved. We ate tuna fish and bologna sandwiches, homemade oatmeal cookies, and if we were lucky, we got some potato chips. We had lemonade or Kool-Aid for drinks and everyone was pleased.

After we finished eating, instead of returning upstairs for the closing song, Aunt Rose raised her arms, got our attention, and we sang, "So long, it's been good to know you . . ."

I did not just get to see Aunt Rose at the Grange Hall, I spent many hours at her farm home with her and Uncle Elwin Churchill. I always felt special when I got to stay overnight with Aunt Rose, because it was only me, and every time I went there, she made me homemade noodles, which was quite a chore.

Uncle Elwin seemed to be retired when I knew him, and he would stare out of a large picture window and watch the trains go by. His little dog sat on his lap, and he also enjoyed watching the cars go by on the road below his house. Sometimes Uncle Elwin told me funny stories when we were eating lunch.

Aunt Rose and Uncle Elwin lived in a two-story wooden house with a white picket fence surrounding it. True to her name, my aunt raised wonderful, fragrant, red and pink roses, which covered their yard.

In the back of her home, there was a large maple tree where I would hook my knees over a limb, let my body drop, and see what the world looked like from upside down. One day, I spotted a large ceramic crock that was about three feet high near the tree. I dropped down to see what was in it. I took off the saucer that was sitting on top and discovered there was lots of fermenting cabbage below the plate. I took a taste of the brine and it was very salty. I decided not to try anymore. I asked her what was inside the pot, and she told me it was homemade sauerkraut. I must have given myself away, because I said, "I don't think it's ready yet."

On one of those nights when I got to sleep over, I realized that Aunt Rose rolled up a long woolen blanket and put it between me and her, all the way down the bed. I asked her why she did that, and she said, "You squirm and kick too much during the night and I need my sleep. It will be fine."

Aunt Rose slept with me to help keep me warm. There wasn't any heat upstairs in their home and it was freezing in the bedroom. She told me, "If you need to go to the bathroom during the night, you have to pull out the pot from underneath the bed and go potty there."

One time, when she wasn't looking, I checked out the pot below my bed. It was made of white enamel and it was as cold as an ice cube. I decided then and there that I would do my best to hold it during the night.

After staying overnight with her during the fall season, I asked my dad, "Why does Aunt Rose have a pot under her bed?"

He quickly answered, "Because they don't have a toilet upstairs in their house."

He didn't want to miss this opportunity to tell me one of his favorite jokes, he said, "Deanna, do you know the difference between a rich man and a poor man?"

I answered, "No."

He went on, "Well, a rich man has a canopy over his bed, and a poor man has a can o'pee under his bed."

I really didn't know what a canopy was at the time, but I gave a half-hearted laugh, because I knew that was what he wanted to hear.

I forgot to tell you that Aunt Rose had a large square metal grate situated right in the middle of the floor of her living room. Warm air blew up from the coal stove that was located in the basement of their house. So, every time I stayed there, I woke up early in the morning and ran down the wooden stairs to stand over the grate. Then, my flannel nightgown billowed up like the hot air balloon I had seen in the picture show. I felt warm and secure.

The grate was nice, but the best thing about going to Aunt Rose's house was that she made me homemade noodles every time I visited her.

Marching Rose Churchill

CHAPTER 4

Sing Your Heart Out!

My mother, Clara, might have been one of the first stage mothers in the United States of America. Especially since she lined up gigs for us at the early ages of eight and five. She found out that I could harmonize at age six, so she had me wrap my arm around my little brother Jimmy's shoulder and sing my heart out at baby showers, wedding showers, and many other gatherings in our small community. I thought nothing of the fact that I could sing two notes above my little brother because we came from a musical family. My dad had his own band where he played the violin and bass fiddle, my mother played the piano, my older brother Dick played the accordion, and my sister Carolyn sometimes sat in for my mother on the piano.

We didn't have television in our rural area, so we spent Sundays visiting other people's homes and having 'jam sessions.' There was always plenty of food too, as everyone brought a dish from home to share with the 'jammers.' At the sessions, my dad's band would play these songs from the fifties. Some are from the twenties, like, "Now is the Hour," "Your Cheating Heart," "Tennessee Waltz," "Roll Out the Barrel," and "In the Mood," just to name a few.

When my dad wasn't farming during the winter months, he would often go on the road with his small band he called Peterschick's Putrid Paralyzers, which was obviously not a classical band. He hired another lady to play the piano so Mom could stay home with the kids. I don't think she wanted the full-time band scene anyway. After playing more of the standards and showing people a good time for three hours, my dad, Bill, would bid everyone farewell with this saying: "Goodnight everyone, and remember, accidents cause people."

Television didn't come to our area until the early fifties, but as soon as we were able to purchase one, we did. It had only a black and white screen that showed mostly snow patterns and a Native American with full regalia. The test pattern seemed to go on for hours. When the shows did come on, I watched *Howdy Doody* and *The Mickey Mouse Club*.

One time, my family watched a local television talent show from KXLY TV called *Starlit Stairway*. It featured local talent, and my mom got the bright idea that Jimmy and I could be on that show and win a prize for our singing talent. The popular song at the time was called "Heart of My Heart." It was just meant for harmonizing, so Mom played it on the piano and we practiced singing it together. I thought we sounded terrific.

The time came for us to drive forty-five minutes to the TV station to try out for *Starlit Stairway*. We did, and the judges must have liked it because we were selected to be on the show.

Can you believe two little kids from Plaza, singing on TV? I thought to myself. *This might be the start of something big. I always wanted to be a singing star like Judy Garland or Deanna Durbin* (the lady for whom I was named).

We drove to Spokane for the rehearsal and I met some of the other performers. I watched them juggle, twirl a baton, and tap dance. They were pretty good, and a lot older than Jimmy and I were. I was nine years old and he was six.

When it was our turn to sing, I stood up straight and tall and put my arm over my little brother's shoulder and belted out "Heart of My Heart." But, alas, at the end of the show the high school girl who swung her baton won the prize and we went home empty-handed. When we went to school after the weekend, the kids who had a TV in their homes ran up to us and said, "We saw you on TV. We saw you sing. You were good. Sorry you did not win anything."

I thought that was the end of my singing career. But the next year, when I was ten and Jimmy was seven, Mom heard the song "This Old House" on the radio and asked me to sing it with Jimmy. I liked the beat a lot, so I belted it out two steps above Jimmy. It looked like the stage lights lit up above my mom's head and she said, "That's it! That's a winner. We are going to try again."

So off we drove to Spokane to audition for *Starlit Stairway* one more time. Evidently, there wasn't a rule about trying out twice for the same show. We made it on again, and this time instead of just standing there with my arm draped over my little brother, I decided to bob up and down to the beat of the music and Jimmy followed my lead. I don't know if it was the combination of our singing or my bright choreography, but we won third prize that time.

We won a trophy and ten dollars. The money helped cover some of the gas we used on our road trips to Spokane. But more than that, we won! I didn't ask Jimmy what he thought about it, but I just knew I was on my way to stardom!

That is, until my best friend's younger cousin Lydia decided to sing a solo in our little room for show and tell. I will never forget what she looked like that day, because she was two years younger than me and I thought she was a lot prettier. She had on a green and black pleated skirt that went just above her knees. On top, she wore a crisp white blouse with a starched collar, and around her neck was a neatly tied black bow made of ribbon. That wasn't the worst part, though. She opened her mouth and she could really sing. I felt my neck turn red with jealousy, as I had never had competition in this area before . . . but right before my eyes, I knew we had a winner in this department. I raised my hands off my lap to clap for her and felt a sense of defeat, as I knew there was a change in the air. We had a new protégé, and it wasn't me.

Deanna and Jimmy Sing their Hearts Out!

CHAPTER 5

The Big Drop

The hardest part of living on the farm for me every summer was waiting for the new school year to begin. That is where I shined. Between my third and fourth grades, I got bored watching the cars go by from the top of my barn. One day, as I was baking in the hot August sun, I came up with a bright idea. Remember when I told you about going to the movies in Rosalia? Well, I thought about the newsreels I saw where thousands of white parachutes floated in the sky toward the ground before landing in Germany. Now, how could I make my own parachute? I figured that the hole where they threw out the hay bales on the barn was high enough and wide enough to jump through. All I needed was a parachute.

I climbed off the roof in a hurry and ran to the farmhouse. Jogging up the stairs, two at a time, I reached the landing to the second floor where our bedrooms were. I couldn't reach the top shelf of my mom's linen cupboard, so I stood on the brass door handle of my bedroom and swung it out toward the hall. Then I propped myself up on the top shelf, where I found the whitest, brightest folded sheet in the cupboard.

I knew my mom was outside in the henhouse, so I pulled it out and let it drop to the floor. Then, I jumped down three feet off the top shelf and landed with a thud. I quickly took the prized possession downstairs and pulled a pair of scissors out of the junk drawer. I thought my mom might come back any minute, so I climbed back up the stairs and took the sheet to my bedroom and locked the door. I had to move fast, so I first cut a large round circle out of the sheet, then poked eight holes around it where I could tie the rope that would go around my waist. Now, where would I get the rope? Of course, from the barn.

I had seen some rope hanging off the rafters, so I tiptoed downstairs and went out the back door. I reached the barn door and picked up the dusty rope that was hanging on a nail in the corner. After shaking the dirt off, I grabbed it and ran back down the path to the house. I crept in quietly and went back upstairs to my bedroom to complete the task. I cut and tied the musty rope to the eight holes, then made a large circle of rope for my waist. I didn't want Mom to see me, so I scrunched the makeshift parachute into a ball and snuck out of the house while she was cutting vegetables for supper.

I thought I was in the clear, but then all of a sudden I heard a small voice, "What are you doing Deanna?"

"Oh, nothing, Jimmy. Why don't you go back to the house and help mom snap peas for the supper. She would love that."

I thought I could talk my five-year-old brother into doing something nice for Mom.

No such luck.

"But I don't want to help Mom. I want to see what you are doing. What is that big thing you have under your shirt?"

I had tried to tuck the parachute out of sight, but it was too late. He saw it.

I knew I wasn't going to be able to get rid of this annoyance of a brother, and I was afraid he might tell my mom.

"Promise you won't tell Mom?"

"I pinky promise," and he grabbed my little finger in a special handshake. A pinky handshake was sacred, and I knew he would keep my secret.

"Okay then. You stay underneath the hayloft window and watch me as I parachute out of the barn. I should go flying and I'll try not to hit you. Back up now as I climb the roof to get to the hayloft."

It took me a while to climb to the top with my large bundle. I was hoping that Jimmy wouldn't get bored and fly off to tell Mother.

"I'm coming, Jimmy. Just wait. I have to tie the ropes around my waist before I jump."

After I adjusted the ropes, I heard a voice yelling, "Fly! Jump out of the hayloft, Deanna."

I glared down at the straw top of my brother's head and screamed back, "Why don't you jump! It's not that easy. It's a long way down to the ground, Jimmy. What if I can't fly? What if this parachute doesn't work?"

"Jump, Deanna, jump!"

I knew I would have to take a flying leap or he would tell everyone at school that I was a chicken. And a chicken, I wasn't.

"Okay, Okay, Jimmy. Hold on, I have to get ready."

I clutched the scratchy side of the window where they tossed hay down to the ground and shoved the round white sheet toward the middle of my back. I gripped the gray shingle and thought to myself, *. . . this is just like the movies when the soldiers jump out of planes and fly away like thousands of white butterflies.*

I suddenly had butterflies in my stomach.

I scooted closer to the edge, and then the front part of my tennis shoe brushed a sliver of lumber loose from the windowsill. I watched it fall feathery to the ground, bouncing like a marshmallow on the soil below, and thought, *I hope I land that easy.*

I took two of the musty ropes I had tied to the circle round my waist and placed one in each hand. I made sure the white sheet was straightened out behind me, then I hollered, "Here I go!"

I felt my whole body catapult into the air and waited for the breeze to open up my parachute.

It did not open!

I splattered onto the silt some eight feet below, hitting the solid ground with my ankles. Then I sprawled out on all fours shrouding my whole being in dust. I was in pain.

After a few seconds, I pushed myself up on my elbows, spit some sand from my mouth and screamed bloody murder, "I broke my leg! I broke my leg! Jimmy, go get Dad!"

Although he sometimes had problems with me, his bossy sister, Jimmy couldn't stand to see me get hurt. The tears gushed down his cheeks and he wailed, "I told you not to jump, Deanna!"

Holding on to my right ankle and swaying back and forth from pain, I cried, "Jimmy, you did not. You told me to jump! I shouldn't have, but . . . just go get Dad."

"Where is he?"

"I think he is behind the barn fixing the combine. Go find him. Now!"

It seemed to be taking some time to find Dad, so while I was waiting, I decided to hold on to my purple ankle. Then I dozed off in the August heat.

"Deanna, wake up!" Someone was nudging my shoulder. I smelled my dad's oily work shirt as he lifted me slowly off the ground with my ankle dangling in the sun.

"Don't move, Deanna. You'll be alright. I think you just sprained your ankle. I'll take you down to the house and we'll put some ice on it."

"You mean my leg's not broken?" I asked.

"I don't think so. We'll check it down at the house."

As he laid me down on our fluffy couch, my mom walked in the room.

"What in the world were you doing, Deanna?"

Not wanting to lie, I blurted out the entire story to her, ending with "... and I am so sorry I ruined your sheet, Mom."

Waiting to hear a reprimand from her, I quickly added, "I really thought I could do it. Maybe I wasn't high enough, or the holes were too big in the parachute, and they let too much air through. I don't know what happened, but I promise I will never do it again. It hurts too much."

Instead of yelling at me, my mom laughed and said, "It's all right Deanna. I used to do stuff like that when I was your age. It's nice to see some creativity in our family. You can snap peas and pick green beans from our garden to help pay off the price of the sheet."

Mom then placed a lightweight blanket over me and said, "Go to sleep now, and get some rest."

I was thankful for what had happened and nodded off smelling my mom's baked spareribs and sauerkraut wafting through the air.

The Big Drop

CHAPTER 6

Give Me That Old Time Religion

Something unusual that changed my life forever also happened the same summer as the Big Drop. My mother decided it was time to have our family go to church, so she asked my father what religion he was supposed to be and he said, "My parents are Catholics, but they don't go to church much anymore. How about you, Clara? What are you supposed to be?"

My mother told him that her family was from North Carolina and they were all raised to be Baptists. She decided to take my dad and attend church at Holy Rosary Catholic Church in Rosalia one Sunday. Since there wasn't a Baptist church in town, they attended the Assembly of God Church the next Sunday. She must have liked the Catholic church better, because she and my dad started taking instructions and joined the church. So, we all joined as well. I attended catechism classes and every summer I would go to summer school at the Catholic church in Malden, Washington. Two nuns conducted the school for two weeks, and it was like going to camp for me and gave me something to do during the summer months. I loved memorizing the Hail Mary and Our Father prayers because I received holy cards if I said them correctly and I would take them home and show them to my parents. I was well on my way to becoming a bona-fide Catholic.

I was very serious about my newfound religion. One time, when I was staying overnight with one of my best friends and her little sister, I asked them, "Have you been baptized?"

They both looked at me a little bewildered, and because of their faces, I determined that they had never been baptized. I read about not being baptized in my catechism book, and because I loved them both so much, I felt I had better do something.

"Don't you know you won't be able to go to heaven unless you are baptized?"

They looked at me with worried expressions, "What do we do then?"

"Get me a bowl full of water and bring it upstairs to the bedroom."

Janice, the older sister, hurried downstairs and brought up a white enamel bowl full of cold water. Looking very proud, she solemnly handed it to me.

Becoming very serious, I said, "Please stand on top of the bed now and I will baptize you."

They climbed on top of the bed, and with a straight face, I dipped my hand into the water and spilled some on each girl's forehead, saying, "I baptize you in the name of the Father, and of the Son, and of the Holy Ghost. Amen."

After it was over, I rested easy knowing my good friends would be able to enter the pearly gates because they were now baptized. After telling a few stories, we three girls snuggled under the covers and fell asleep for the night.

Being of a German background, all of my friends at Plaza Grade School were either Methodist or Lutheran. We were the only Catholic family at school, and sometimes, when kids were mad at me for being too bossy, they said, "You're Catholic!" and I would answer, "So what?!"

Calling me names only tended to make me stronger in my faith.

One of the things I was sad about during my grade school years was that I could not join the Rainbow Girls. All my friends were in this organization, and when they reached the upper grades, they went to formal dances with boys from the DeMolay group and I could not join them. Catholics were forbidden to join the Freemasons and Eastern Star organization because of religious reasons, and Rainbow Girls and DeMolay boys' groups were connected to the Freemasons. No one ever explained to me why I could not belong. I just wanted to dress up and go to the dances with my friends. My first inklings of feeling left out started there.

AND WE ALL GO TO HEAVEN, BY SELAH YOUNG

CHAPTER 7
The Music Man Cometh and Goeth

A s you might recall from earlier chapters, my family was really into music. So, it was big news when I entered the fifth grade because we were going to have a visiting band teacher come to our small school and teach us how to play instruments. This was the first time Plaza Grade School ever had a special teacher for music.

We were all seated in the 'big room' waiting for the new teacher to arrive when in popped a short man with balding hair and wire-rimmed glasses propped up on his short, turned-up nose.

He wore a tweed suit and a bow tie, something I would expect from a music teacher. He was very prepared for our first day of band and told us his name was Mr. Snobgrain. Now, I thought that was a rather funny name in the first place, but it also fit his looks. His first job was to figure out what kind of instruments we wanted to play, so he put on a demonstration for us. He played the saxophone, the clarinet, the trumpet, and the trombone. Then, he showed us how to play the drums. He told us he would have someone play the piano for us if we needed it for our band.

We then signed up to have our parents rent the instruments from a music store in Spokane. After hearing Mr. Snobgrain play the alto saxophone, I decided that was the instrument I wanted to play. Besides, it was gold and the clarinets were black, not my favorite color. We had to wait for him to return the next week before we could get our instruments . . . and it was a very long week for me.

The days passed, and it was finally time to have our first day of band practice. The practice was held on the cement floor below the classrooms, the same place where we played basketball. There was only one small window along the top part of the concrete brick wall, so there wasn't a lot of light down there and it was very chilly. The coldness of the room did not take away from the excitement I felt when I opened the case and saw my shiny brass saxophone. I knew we were going to be friends forever.

Mr. Snobgrain had to help everyone place the bamboo reeds on the clarinets and the saxophones before a note was played. We all listened and paid attention. We didn't want to get kicked out of band class on the first day.

He told us to lick the reed before we placed it on the mouthpiece and to tighten the reed once we had it in the right place. That way, it wouldn't fall off in the middle of a song.

Then, he had to tell the drummers to quit hitting their sticks on the drums because he wanted us to hear what he had to say about playing an actual song.

There were about ten of us in grades five and six in the band. Our first notes sounded pretty bad, but after a few weeks we sounded better. The first two songs we learned were "Go Tell Aunt Rhodie" and "Mary Had a Little Lamb."

There wasn't enough room in our school to hold a band concert where friends and family could attend, so our first concert was held in the Grange hall across the street from our school. There was a stage where we placed our chairs and set the music stands in front of us. There were over fifty people in the crowd the night of the spring concert, and many of them were my relatives. I was a bit nervous, because if you hit the wrong note playing the saxophone it really stands out because it is so loud.

Mr. Snobgrain had combed a few pieces of his hair over to the side of his head and was all dressed up in his finest gray suit. He was also wearing his polished black patent leather shoes for the performance.

He stood in front of us and raised his baton. Out came the blaring sounds of a beginning band and the rat-a-tat-tat of the drums as we played "Go Tell Aunt Rhodie." The crowd loved it and gave us a hearty round of applause. We even had an encore piece ready, so we played "On Top of Old Smoky," which everyone knew. It was a great night and I thought I was ready to join a group like Tommy Dorsey's band that my dad always talked about.

Speaking of my dad, he was talking to our neighbor Donny about the new band teacher and he asked him how he liked the band. Donny answered, "I like it a lot."

"What instrument do you play, Donny?"

"I play the trumpet," he proudly proclaimed.

"Well, what notes do you play on the trumpet?" Dad asked.

"I play A, B, C, D, E, F, G, and H," Donny responded.

"But Donny, there is no H." my dad calmly replied.

Donny raised his shoulders, looked at my dad, and said, "Well, I play it."

Something happened at the end of the year, because Mr. Snobgrain left for greener pastures. Perhaps he heard too many H notes!

Well, I Play it!

PART TWO

Intermediate Years

CHAPTER 8

The Scary Teacher

I began the fifth grade at Plaza Grade School after my summer of trying to fly. Now there were three girls and three boys in my class. This made it easy for any teacher to pair us up for games. I knew there was a change in the air because Mr. and Mrs. Ronald had moved on and were no longer our teachers. I felt a sense of loss, especially when I had the first glimpse of my new teacher.

It was a man. It seemed like all the teachers in the upper grades, five through eight, were always men. I guess they thought a fragile woman couldn't handle the older kids, but I would have preferred the gentleness of a female teacher over what we got that year.

The new teacher wore a striped suit that was too big for his frame. He was also wearing a blue and yellow squiggly tie. He introduced himself as Mr. Falcon. The thing is, he actually looked like a falcon. He had a pointed nose and a square jaw, and he stared at us with dark, beady, brown eyes. His teeth stuck out of his mouth in an overbite and they were stained with a gold color. When he bent down to tell me something about my schoolwork, I smelled cigarette breath. Maybe that was why he had stained, brown teeth.

What he looked like could have been forgiven if he was in any way kind to us. He taught us in a strict manner, and when he spoke to us, his dark brown eyes flittered back and forth like he was trying to find something. Everyone in grades five through eight towed the line and paid attention when he spoke. We tried to learn our math, social studies, reading, and writing despite the stern looks.

If that was all that happened, I could finish my story right here. But it was not.

Mr. Falcon had short bursts of temper that were not reasonable. When we were standing in line to get a drink of water at the water fountain and we looked at him the wrong way, he grabbed our arm and sent us back to the classroom.

One day, when we were waiting in the water line, one of my closest friends named Darlene was standing behind me. She had curly auburn hair and freckles, and if you smiled at her, she blushed and her cheeks turned red. She never spoke out in class and always did everything the teachers told her to do. Mr. Falcon suddenly grabbed her for no reason and pushed her down on the hard wooden floor. I couldn't believe what I was seeing, and I didn't know what to do. I felt tears come to my eyes but I didn't dare say anything or I knew that he would push me down, too. Darlene got up and ran back to the classroom holding her breath in case he came after her again.

When the bell rang and recess was over, we all walked back into the classroom in a quiet daze. Everyone in the class thought, *Why Darlene, of all the students? Not sweet Darlene.* She had her head down on her desk as we walked into the room. With tear-stained eyes, she eventually sat up to face the hawk standing in front of us. You could hear a pin drop the rest of the afternoon, and the incident was so bizarre none of us wanted to talk about it.

I did tell my mother about what Mr. Falcon did to Darlene, and she said, "Deanna, Mr. Falcon just came back from the war and I think he suffers from shell shock. I will talk to the president of the school board about it tomorrow and see what they will do."

Evidently, the school board president had a stern discussion with Mr. Falcon, as he never laid a hand on any of us kids again. But he did leave after only one year of teaching.

CHAPTER 9

From a Country Mouse
to a City Girl

The next year, when I went into the sixth grade, something happened that changed my life forever. My sister, Carolyn, was in high school and was 'sowing her oats,' as they say. She and her girlfriend took my mom and dad's car out for a spin in the wheat fields behind our house without their permission. She was not on the road, so I don't know why my mom got so mad. She scolded her and told her that she was going to send her away to boarding school in Spokane. I was crying and holding on to my sister's leg, begging my mom not to send her away, but she did.

She sent her to Saint Bernadette Academy, where she finished her last two years of high school. Carolyn came home on some weekends, but she lived in the dorms at the school during the week. I missed her terribly. There wasn't anyone to help me do my chores or to tell me funny stories at night to help me go to sleep.

I think my mom thought she was doing the right thing, because Catholic schools had a good reputation for teaching students and emphasizing the arts. Carolyn was being trained to play classical pieces on the piano and she was good at it. Being at the Academy allowed her to participate in the orchestra and accompany the choir. I still missed her.

Then came the next jolt. Not only was Carolyn gone, but two years after she left, my mom and dad sat Jimmy and me down and told us that they were selling the farm and moving to Spokane so we could attend Catholic schools. What? Leave the farm?! What about my best friend and neighbor, Claire Hoff, and what about my girlfriends who lived far out in the country? What about my boy cousins and possible boyfriends? I was not happy, but it did not seem like there was anything I could do about it. I resigned myself to a new adventure.

My parents enrolled us in Saint Alphonse Elementary School located near a large university. I was in the eighth grade and Jimmy was in the fifth grade.

I remember the first day of school, and instead of five people in my class, there were twenty-five students and my teacher was a nun named Sister MaryAnne. She wore a traditional black and white habit, and I immediately looked under her white starched bonnet to see if I could see any hair. I always heard that women shaved their heads when they became a nun.

The students were friendly to me, mostly because they were curious. I guess I did some things in an odd way, because Sister MaryAnne sent me to the hall while she talked to the students. I was very concerned about what she was saying.

She brought me back into the classroom, and we continued our studies. Being surprised about the incident, I asked one of my new friends, "What did she say about me in there?"

Feeling sorry for me, my friend Patty said, "Sister MaryAnne told us that you might do things a little differently than we do because you are coming from the country and might not know our ways. She also said you might talk in an odd way, as well."

That really made me feel strange, but I did know that some of my grammar was not the same as the city folks. Following my mother's lead, I said things like, "He done it," and "she seen it."

I didn't even know that wasn't the way to talk until I got a workbook about grammar from Sister MaryAnne and she asked me to study it. I also took the workbook home to my mom and said she should study it, as well.

One of the things I liked about Saint Alphonse was the fact that there were more boys to pal around with. I also was selected to be a cheerleader for the boys' basketball games when they played against other parochial schools in Spokane. I was not the best at cheerleading, but I had a long ponytail and I was in my glory.

PART THREE

High School
and
College Years

CHAPTER 10

My Turn for the Academy

After feeling like a big deal at Saint Alphonse, my mom signed me up to attend Saint Bernadette Academy for the following four years. It was my turn to take my sister's place. At least I did not have to stay there every night.

By this time, my mom had gotten a job at Spokane General Hospital working in the Central Supply Department, where she prepared instruments for surgeries and other medical procedures. My dad was still driving truck for the county so they could afford the $600 tuition to have me attend the Academy.

There was only one big hitch: there were no boys at this school! We also had to wear these ugly green jumpers with a white blouse for uniforms. First of all, I had liked going to school with boys and appreciated their company; especially when they noticed me in the halls at Saint Alphonse and pulled my ponytail or made me laugh in the middle of class as we tried to hide our giggles from Sister MaryAnne.

Secondly, there were no boys' baseball, football, or basketball games to cheer for. The girls cheered for the girls, and if you played on one of the teams, as I did for basketball, you did not get to cheer at all. And lastly, the girls at Saint Bernadette's had a social club called Touma, and you had to be selected to join the club.

The problem was I didn't know how to get into this select club. The girls who were my friends from Saint Alphonse knew the ropes, or they had older sisters or friends who helped them join the club, and they got in. My former friends now stuck together during lunch and sat at a special table set aside just for the girls who belonged to Touma. They also wore a gold necklace with a T on it to identify them as being a Touma girl. No sign on the table that said we could not sit there; we just knew it was only for a select few.

I was only fourteen years old when I suddenly felt 'less than,' and I wasn't used to the feeling. When my close friends from Saint Alphonse all got 'in' their freshman year, I did some checking around to find out more about this club. What I found was not so pretty. I don't know the exact process, but I heard from some of the other girls who did not get selected that the older girls had a special wooden device. They would say the name of an underclass girl and talk about her. Then, each girl would take a white marble and roll it down the device if they wanted the girl to be in Touma. If one girl selected a black marble and rolled it down, the girl would not be chosen and was considered to be 'blackballed.' I must have been 'blackballed,' because I did not get asked to belong or given a gold chain to wear around my neck. I was only fourteen and devastated, because all of my friends from Saint Alphonse had been selected, but not me.

Just like the feeling I had about Rainbow Girls, I felt left out once again. Sure enough, my once-close friends sat together at the special table and the 'wannabes' like me gathered together and picked a table in the corner to sit at and pretend it didn't bother us. But it did . . . especially me, as they had been my friends at Saint Alphonse Elementary School.

I started thinking, *What is wrong with me? Did I not roll my socks down just right? Was my slip showing under my uniform? Should I have talked to one of the older girls and asked them how to get in?* Then I decided that maybe I could figure out how to do this on my own and be chosen in my sophomore year. But sophomore year came and went, and none of my new friends nor I were selected to join Touma. I always figured that all of us were in the middle group of sort of popular, but not so popular. I didn't dwell on it too much until the Touma girls sponsored a formal dance to be held at the Ritz Hotel in downtown Spokane. Some of my old friends asked me to help them sell tickets for the dance and I gladly obliged, thinking it might help me get 'in' the next year. That did not happen, or the year after that.

My thought is that some people in clubs like this want to feel a little bit higher than those who want to get 'in.' Otherwise it wouldn't be fun if you weren't one of the 'cool ones' with a gold necklace around your neck and had your own table at lunchtime. Where were the boys when I needed them? I always got along well with boys.

Compensating for my lack of being one of the 'most popular girls,' I delved into my studies and joined the school choir called Triple Trio. Remember, I could harmonize, so I was selected to participate as an alto. In fact, the Triple Trio was invited to join other high school choirs and sing at the Spokane Coliseum, where we performed Handel's *Messiah* for a large audience. It was a 'joyful' experience.

In addition, I became an honor student and received slips to take home to my parents showing them my high grades in various subjects. I really never shared my hurt feelings with my mom and dad because they worked so hard, and I didn't want to bother them. Besides, by the time I was a senior, I had formed my own group of friends and I knew how to have fun with them. When I graduated, I was not the valedictorian or salutatorian, but I was academically tenth in my class of ninety girls.

It was not all bad at Saint Bernadette's. One of the highlights of my years there was when the nuns hired a drama teacher named Darla

Swan to teach us how to act in real plays. I not only liked her classy name, but I was also fascinated with her slim figure, her fluffy reddish hair, and her black wire-rimmed glasses. I was so used to seeing the nuns in their black and white habits, or 'penguin uniforms' as some of us called them, that it was nice to see someone in street clothes. Darla Swan had been a real actress at one time, and she knew a lot about teaching drama. She taught us all the parts of the stage and made sure we knew where to go when she yelled, "Go downstage left."

Also, we had to audition for our parts like real actresses and show Darla Swan our 'stuff.'

We put on the play of the *Wizard of Oz*, and I was selected to play the coveted role of the Wicked Witch of the West. I practiced that laugh and really got it down. In fact, we put the play on for some little kids in Spokane, and when I did the laugh, some of them started crying. I felt kind of bad, but I couldn't help it, as it was my part. Looking back, my witch laugh served me well over the years, and when I attended class reunions, my friends always asked me to do the witch's cackle.

To their credit, the Benedictine sisters were devoted to their work of teaching God's children. In general, I had excellent teachers, but a few of them were a little goofy. We had one nun who was getting rather old and she had crooked teeth. She used to physically show us how she did ballet when she was a young girl. She would pick up her habit and do a few twirls right there in the classroom, and since she was rather chubby, it caused us to snicker. Her large round eyes got big and her face turned bright red with anger when we giggled. Spittle would be coming out of the side of her mouth as she yelled, "Who is doing that snickering?"

Then she ran down the aisle to find out who the culprits were, and the girls who were doing it would suddenly quit. Then the girls on the other side of the room started cackling and she would run to that side. All the while, the rest of us would be stifling our guffaws in case we got in trouble. Since she could never figure out what was happening, the next time she showed us her pirouette, we started humming and she would run down from one side to the other to find out who was making the noise. We did this a few times to break the boredom in her classroom. I really think that she was a little unstable and ready for retirement, but saints we were not!

As a footnote, a few years after I left Saint Bernadette Academy, the Bishop of the Diocese outlawed Touma there. Not only me, but he and his committee felt it was not an appropriate organization for a Catholic school, which is known to promote social justice. Thank God!

St. Bernadette's

CHAPTER 11

More of the Same
and the Break Away

I don't know why I agreed, but Mom thought I should go to Saint Bernadette's College instead of another university. It was right across the street from the Academy and she could drive me there and drop me off for classes before she headed up to her job at Spokane General Hospital. Since I was going to stay at home, it would also be less expensive than having me attend Eastern Washington University or Washington State University, where I would have to pay for room and board. I thought, *Oh no, more girls again.* For some reason, I decided to make the most of it and I determined that I was going to be popular and take an active part in the activities at Saint Bernadette's College. I had watched enough girls in high school to decide that I was not a country girl anymore, and I knew how to work the system. I got enough dates with guys on my own, so that wasn't really the problem. I became the president of the Day Students (what we called the women who commuted to school, there were fifty of us in the group) and a member of the student council at Saint Bernadette's College. I brought donuts and maple bars to the meetings. I knew the way to the heart was through the stomach. One time, the principal from the Academy came to visit the college, and she stopped me in the hall and said, "Deanna, you really have blossomed over here."

I thought to myself, *I was already a flower before I came here, but not everyone knew how to gather the petals.*

I attended classes and found that I was very proficient in learning the German language. Sister Marie Jane, who was my singing teacher at the Academy, took German with me and we became friends instead of teacher and student. I was an adult now and I had to act like one.

While I was attending Saint Bernadette College, the nuns decided to buy some property in Fort Wayne on the other side of town and move the college to that location. It was a great place for people who resided at the college because they lived in the quarters of former officers who had lived there when it was a working fort and military post. Our college changed its name to Fort Wayne College and my dad started driving me to and from the school. I didn't have my own car, so I was happy to have him along for the ride.

While at Fort Wayne, I was inducted into the SPURS National Honor Society for sophomore women. The name stands for service, patriotism, unity, responsibility, and sacrifice. The organization was founded at Montana State University in 1922 and spread to other smaller colleges and universities across the United States. I was elected as the vice president of our group at Fort Wayne. At one point, we attended a large gathering of over three hundred SPURS at the University of Idaho, and we stayed in sorority houses on the campus in Moscow, Idaho. It seemed to me that living in a sorority would be a lot of fun based on my experiences at the University of Idaho.

While I commuted to Fort Wayne, I also started working as a sales clerk at Sears in downtown Spokane. I did this on the weekends when I wasn't going to classes, and I started to earn my own money. I sold men's clothes in the basement of the store. I remember wearing high heels every day so I would look good when selling the clothes. It must have worked, because I was the top salesperson for two months in a row.

Getting my own money propelled me to think about moving to a co-ed college in the fall. I saved up enough to pay for tuition, room, and board at Eastern Washington University. I had always dreamed of attending Washington State University when I grew up in the Palouse country, but my parents couldn't afford to send me there, so I became an Eastern Eagle. I wanted to experience living in a dorm, so I resided at Lorenz Hall in Cheney, Washington.

I found my calling . . . and did I have fun. At one point, I was being a little feisty and I purchased a blinking red lantern for my dorm room. One spring evening, I decided to turn it on and shine it out of my dorm window. Some boys lived in the circular building across from our dorm and they must have seen it blinking. Thinking it meant what it was supposed to mean, they came running down the hill and raided our hall. They took lingerie from the laundry rooms, knocked on our doors, and headed back home. We all thought it was funny since it was a hot spring night, and we were tired of studying anyway.

It was not so hilarious the next day when I was summoned to the Dean of Students' office to fess up to my transgression. One of the boys who was the ringleader of the invasion was also called to the Dean's office. He was also a friend of mine, and when the Dean asked him why he and some other boys raided our dorm, he said it was his idea and he never mentioned the blinking red light. That gallant young man really had my back. Thank the good Lord, I finally went to school with boys.

PART FOUR

Grown-Up Years

CHAPTER 12

The Value of Being Bilingual

German was my major in college so I studied it vigorously and received all As in the class. I never realized how important knowing the language would be until I got to use it. A friend of mine who was in my German class at Eastern called me on the phone and said, "Deanna, my cousin is coming over from Germany and I would like to have my girlfriend and I go on a double date, but he can't speak English. I know you can speak it, so would you consider going out with him and speaking German to him for the night? I know that is a lot to ask, but I think you can do it."

"Sure, Hans. I will give it a try, but you'll have to get a date for my friend because she is staying overnight with me. It will have to be a triple date."

"Okay. I will find someone to go out with your friend. See you Friday night," he replied.

Friday night came and the car pulled into my driveway. Hans and his girlfriend were in the front seat, and after introducing me to his cousin, Willie, Hans had me slide in next to him in the backseat. Hans then had my friend Jean sit next to me, and a young man named Rick Gilmore sat next to Jean on the outside.

I didn't have time to worry about how my friend was getting along with Rick Gilmore because I was busy trying to speak German to Willie on my side of the car. It was difficult because native speakers speak faster than German learners like me, and it was all I could do to keep up with the conversation.

Willie was kind of good looking, with wavy blonde hair, and I wanted to make a good impression so I tried my hardest.

Deanna: Hallo, Ich bin Deanna. (*Hello, I am Deanna*) Wo kommen Sie her? (*Where do you come from?*)

Willie: Ich komme aus Heidelberg. (*I come from Heidelberg.*)

And so the night went. I was struggling to speak German, and Willie was trying to understand my broken Deutsch. I knew I was not going to see him again, so I wasn't too worried about it.

Meanwhile, my friend's date, Rick Gilmore, proceeded to have too many beers and he kept coming to sit by me instead of paying attention to her. As he got more tipsy, we ended up leaving Rick at the local college hangout and driving off without him. I did not know what I was going to say to Jean that night, and I had no idea what Hans would say to his friend, Rick. I did not want to know, really.

I thought that was the last I would see of Rick Gilmore, but sure enough, a few weeks later some of my girlfriends from Eastern wanted to go to that same pub to celebrate finishing our finals. About six of us sat down around a table, and the next thing you know, a familiar face comes and sits right next to me. It was that inconsiderate Rick Gilmore, who had obviously been drinking, but right in front of all the other girls he said, "You are the prettiest girl I have ever seen."

Everyone heard him and my face turned fifty shades of red, but underneath it all, I felt flattered. He stayed and talked to me for a while and that was that.

My next encounter with Mr. Gilmore happened three weeks later at the same pub. I saw one of my girlfriends from the Academy, who was sitting at a table with her date, so I sat down across from them and started talking. Sure enough, who slid into the empty chair next to me? You guessed it. Rick Gilmore. Evidently, he knew both of these people before I came along and he wasn't drinking. My Academy friend and her date invited Rick and me to play a game with them. The friends I had come with were busy doing something else, so I agreed. We played the States game, where you name a state and the next person has to name a state starting with the last letter of the first state's name. Ex. Alaska, (next) Alabama. This went on for a while until we ran out of states to name. Rick left the table and my Academy friend said, "Deanna, he is really a nice guy when he isn't drinking."

Quite an endorsement, but it was in the back of my mind when I got a phone call that next Sunday.

"Hi, Deanna. Do you remember me? I'm Rick Gilmore and we played the States game the other night. I was wondering if you would like to go to a drive-in movie with me tonight?"

I had to think fast, as it was a Sunday. There was a blue law in effect in Washington on Sundays and no one was allowed to buy alcohol, so I said, "Yes, I'll go."

He was kind of cute after all, and Sundays were slow days for me.

Rick came to pick me up and he seemed kind of nervous. He sat across from my father and placed his hands on the sides of this big green Naugahyde chair and answered my dad's questions. "Yes, Mr. Peterschick."

"No, Mr. Peterschick."

I think I fell in love with him right then and there before we ever left the house. He looked so handsome, vulnerable, and sober!

Rick and Deanna's Engagement Photo

CHAPTER 13

Two Become One

Rick and I 'hit it off,' as they say, so he decided to attend college at Eastern to be with me. After living in the dorm, I decided to rent an apartment with my girlfriend instead of living there. I was a senior and Rick was a sophomore. I didn't find this out until we were in separate lines to sign up for classes. I suddenly had doubts about our relationship, but I was too far gone by then to care.

We dated the next year and were married on August 14, 1965, at Saint Rose of Lima Church in Cheney, Washington. It was a small church that held one hundred people. It was a terrific day and we had a reception in the Cheney Community Hall. We couldn't afford to have a dance, so after the meal Rick and I left for our honeymoon in our hometown, Spokane. Rick ran into a high school friend of his in the lobby and introduced me to him. He said, "This is my wife, Deanna." That had a nice ring to it.

The next day, we headed to Westminster, California, where I had signed a contract to teach. We wanted a new adventure, and California paid more for new teachers. My contract was $5,700 for a full year of teaching second grade. Rick hadn't finished college yet, so he got a job selling Pet Milk to grocery stores in the area. He was required to drive on the busy freeways all over Los Angeles and Orange County, California. He developed a phobia about driving in heavy traffic and something else happened that altered our plans for staying in Orange County.

Being Catholics (Rick took instructions before we got married and became a Catholic) we were supposed to use the rhythm method. Evidently, our rhythm was out of sync, and I became pregnant the very month we were married. I was sure people would count the months since we were so close to our wedding date; but we were married on August 14, 1965, and our baby was born on June 7, 1966 . . . nine months and three weeks after our marriage.

We were not planning on having a baby so soon, but we were delighted with our firstborn, who weighed a whopping nine pounds, six ounces. We named him Patrick Hale, and his middle name was his grandmother's maiden name. He had big dimples, and Rick and I stared at him for hours as he laid between us in the bed.

I nursed Patrick, so I brought him to bed with us. While I was feeding him, Patrick pushed down on my breast and milk squirted in the air. Rick was very alarmed, "Deanna, I think he has a leak."

After laughing a while, I told him, "No, he is just pushing his hand down on me. He is fine."

Life went along quite well, as I was able to stay home and take care of Patrick. We had decided to leave Southern California while I was home on maternity leave because there were too many people there for us, and after working for Pet Milk and driving all over Southern California, Rick didn't want any more heavy traffic. He still had to finish his college degree, so we decided to move to Bellingham, Washington, where he could pursue his bachelor's degree in teaching at Western Washington University. I applied for a teaching job at Median Elementary and I was hired. I was happy that I wouldn't have to start teaching until the fall, as Patrick was my first baby and I would find it hard to leave him.

I found a babysitter for Patrick over the summer months and she was a stay-at-home mom. She also lived just a short way from the school where I would teach fourth grade. An ideal situation as, unbeknownst to the babysitter and my husband, I planned on driving to the babysitter's home during my short noon hour to nurse my little baby. That only lasted a little while because our lunch hour was so short and it was stressful to get everything done before I had to go back to school.

I enjoyed my two years at Median, but the first year I had to teach in the room beneath the gym. Every time a class had recess during the cooler months, they would come to the gym to play basketball. I might be teaching an important concept in math, and all of the sudden we heard bouncing balls over our heads and the students could barely hear me teach. In the second year, they found a better classroom for me and it was much nicer. My fourth-grade students performed a play for their parents, and I realized that this was a great way to learn how to read, speak, and gain confidence. After the play's success, I knew that I would always include drama in my teaching from then on.

It was also during the fall of my second year of teaching that I realized I was going to have another baby. But luckily, the baby was due during the spring and I could take off the summer months to stay home and nurse whoever it would turn out to be. There was a 50 percent chance it was a boy or a girl.

We did not find out the baby's sex ahead of time, so when our second baby was born, we were delighted to welcome a baby girl. She weighed eight pounds and five ounces, and she was gorgeous with tiny hands and feet, and on top of her head was a mess of dark auburn hair. I wondered where that came from and I remembered that Rick was Irish and when he grew out his sideburns they were red, as well.

We thought we were being very clever to name her Amy, as we hadn't heard that name very often. Lo and behold, the name mushroomed like a field of weeds, and in just a few years every other girl had the name Amy. We felt blessed to have a child of each gender and they were both very healthy.

One of the teachers at Median asked if we wanted to rent their log cabin in Bellingham. We had been living in a basement apartment underneath another family in Lynden, Washington, and while they were wonderful landlords, we thought we might like to have a house of our own.

Believe it or not, Iris and Lyle Born rented the two-bedroom log house to us for forty dollars a month. They wanted to help young couples just starting out in the world. They had one son named Larry who was already out on his own, so they took us in like mother hens guarding their nest. They also had us over for dinner every weekend, where we sat down to wonderful roast beef, potatoes, and gravy or fried chicken and potatoes and gravy, followed by a homemade raspberry pie.

I was quite content in our log house, and when I returned to teaching in the fall, I had a new, wonderful babysitter for my two children. Her name was Maureen Darting, and she was one of the kindest young mothers I had ever met. She was just a little older than me, so she taught me a lot about raising little ones. She and herhusband, James, had two boys named John and Jacob, and a spunky little girl named Jane. The Dartings lived just a few steps away from our log home, so it was very convenient to drive my children to her home every day. She and James became our close friends and we were able to do a few things together, such as go to movies and out to dinner. The main thing I knew was that Maureen would be good to my children while I was teaching, and this indeed proved to be the case. She and her children became very close to Pat and Amy during those two years we were in Bellingham. Good landlords, a comfortable and inexpensive home, a great teaching job, and a wonderful babysitter. What more could I have wanted as a working mother?

CUTTING CAKE AT OUR WEDDING

CHAPTER 14

Pow! Right in the Kisser

"**P**ow! Right in the kisser."

This was an expression that Jackie Gleason used on his television show, *The Honeymooners*, which was popular at the time. He used the saying as if he would like to do this to his wife when she upset him . . . but which, of course, he never did. That was how I felt when Rick came home one day from college and said, "Deanna, why don't we teach in Alaska? I went to the job fair today at school and I talked to some people from the Bureau of Indian Affairs (BIA) about teaching there. I always wanted to go to Alaska. They pay our way and everything."

I replied, "Are you serious? Why would I want to move with you to Alaska with Pat and Amy, especially when I love my job at Median and I have such a good babysitter for our kids? You have to be out of your mind if you think I will move up there with you."

He went on trying to persuade me with some more of the facts. "But Deanna, teaching couples who teach in remote villages for the Bureau of Indian Affairs make more money than they do down here. I think they start at $25,000 each. Do you realize that with that kind of money, we would be able to go up there for one year, come back, and buy a house?"

Well, that DID sound interesting. Every woman wants her own home to nest in and decorate. And he did say that we would only have to stay for one year. After one year in the villages, we would come back to Bellingham and buy a house. Bellingham was a great little city, and at least we would have enough money saved to put a down payment on a home. We had many friends in Bellingham, and if we moved back after one year, this wouldn't be such a bad idea . . . But, I still had a pit in my stomach and was sick at the thought of leaving my teaching job, our landlords, and our babysitter. I certainly was not sure of anything.

Rick said, "Well, here are some brochures for you to look through and some more information about the BIA. There are also some contracts in here for us to sign in case we decide to do this. You can take your time, but I really want to go. Don't you?"

Not wanting to squelch his enthusiasm, I meekly said, "I'll look it over."

Now, mind you, I did not sleep that night or the next, or the next. I was pretty upset, and every day Rick would try to talk me into going. I knew he was quite the adventurer because he spent a year traveling in Europe before he met me. He had the wandering bug, but I didn't.

After three or four days of cajoling and promising me that the Bureau of Indian Affairs would take care of us, and that I wouldn't have to worry about anything, and reminding me that we could buy a house after one year in Alaska, I relented to his desires and reluctantly said, "Yes."

Rick was elated and I was terrified! Who was going to take care of my precious children while I was earning that $25,000 to go toward my house? What if they got sick or injured? Where did you take them to the doctor when you were out on the tundra? What if I got sick or injured? Who would become my substitute teacher? Who would take care of my children when Rick was teaching? And on and on ...

Luckily, we had a few months to get used to the idea, as we applied shortly after Amy was born and didn't hear back from the BIA for a while. I had a mixed reaction when we received our acceptance letter in the mail. I was placed at a higher general schedule (GS) rating than Rick, which is the level the government uses to rank their employees. This was because I had three years of teaching experience and Rick was just starting his career. When I saw the GS-9 on my contract and GS-7 on his, at least I felt I had received recognition for my few years of teaching. As a woman growing up in the sixties during the feminist movement, I also felt a bit of pride in having a higher salary than my husband.

What did we need to do to get prepared? We had to put all of our furniture and goods into storage. We would have no need for any of those items up there, as the living quarters and furniture were provided to us by the BIA. How would we get food up there?

The BIA had sent us a set of manifests telling us all the things we needed to do, and with it came a set of ordering sheets for our food ... food that had to last for a year. I hardly managed knowing what to buy at the grocery store for two days, let alone for one year. I fastidiously looked over the bill of lading and marked the supplies I would need, noting that I would not be able to purchase fresh milk, fresh produce, or fresh meat from any source. All the food we ordered had to be in the form of a can or in a box. The BIA would fill the order in Seattle and ship everything up on the North Star, a huge ship that would dock near Kotzebue, Alaska. From there, they would send the goods to the villages by barge.

When August 1968 arrived, we packed our personal belongings, diaper bag, clothes, and a few other odds and ends. We put our major furniture in storage, preparing to pick it up in one year when we returned to Bellingham with money in hand to buy a new house. Our babysitter, Maureen Darting, and two of her children drove us to Seattle to pick up our three-hour flight to Anchorage via Alaska Airlines. There were many hugs and embraces as we left our friends. When I turned around to wave goodbye, I saw Maureen's oldest boy with a bucket of tears rolling down his face. That brought a flood of tears to my eyes as I walked through the sliding glass door to our new life.

PART FIVE

Alaska Years

CHAPTER 15

A Fish Out of Water

I had never flown to Alaska before, let alone with two little babies in tow. I wanted to look great for the flight, so I bought a gray suede coat with a gray fur collar to wear on the plane. Being young and not so practical, I also wore matching gray high heels so I looked spectacular for the three-hour flight.

I remember going to the gate when our plane number was called and saw that the plane was quite full. Rick and I both had babies on our hips as we waited in line. Rick carried Pat, who was also dressed to the nines, with his little beige cap on the top of his head. I carried Amy with her beautiful auburn hair peeking from underneath her pink knitted cap. We were quite the family of four flying to Alaska for the first time.

More and more people boarded the plane in front of us. Rick, being a polite man, told some people they could go ahead of us as we were trying to cajole our children into being quiet. When we finally arrived at the gate with our tickets in hand, the departure warden said, "We are so sorry. The plane was overbooked and we have no more seats. We will have to put you on another plane tomorrow morning."

Are you kidding? I was so mad at Rick for being so kind and letting people go in front of us. Did this mean that we would be one whole day late for our training for the BIA? What would we do now? How would we get to a hotel and back for our next flight? The kids were tired already; how would they feel sleeping in a strange bed and going through all of this again?

I had always heard that if you missed your flight, someone from the airlines would promptly take care of you. They would help you with your children and make sure everything was pleasant while you waited for your next plane.

No such luck for us. The gate shut and the ticket agents closed up their desks and walked away. We were left standing with two crying babies on our hips and no place to go. Where was all this help we were supposed to have? Rick knew I wasn't too happy with him, so he told me to sit down with the two babies, and he would go to the main desk to sort things out. Luckily, I was nursing Amy, so I was able to quiet her down while we waited for Daddy to come back and save us.

After a few minutes, Rick returned to the boarding area and told me they would put us up overnight in a hotel in Seattle. He said they would also give us some vouchers for a taxi to bring us to the hotel and back in the morning for our flight to Alaska. What a great way to start our trip. The other teachers would already be settled in and we would just be arriving. I thought, *Oh well, at least they paid for everything and we would eventually get there.* I had to practice some patience.

After a restless night in a downtown hotel in Seattle, a taxi picked us up and we made another departure for the airline company. We boarded the plane this time, and again, I wore my gray high heels and beautiful suede coat with the gray fur collar. We were on our way.

After two and a half hours of flying, we looked down at the breath-taking snow-capped mountains over the Anchorage area. It was sunny and clear that day, and the sight was breathtaking. Maybe this Alaska adventure wasn't going to be so bad after all. Nature has a way of securing these feelings.

We finally arrived in Anchorage, where we then transferred to a Wien Airlines Twin Otter plane on our way to Sitka, Alaska. Sitka, a fishing village that had been settled by the Tlingit Indians, was surrounded by water. You could only get there by boat or plane. Even though it had a small population, it had one of the largest ports and was known for its commercial fishing enterprises.

Once we flew to Sitka, they sent us on a smaller plane to Mount Edgecumbe Boarding School, which was located on Kruzof Island. The Bureau of Indian Affairs ran the school, but since it was August, the students were not there. It was a good place for the new teachers to live while they were being trained to teach in remote villages.

Rick had called the BIA when we were in Seattle to let them know we had missed our plane and that we would be arriving a day late. Someone from the BIA told us there would be a school bus on the island to pick us up and bring us to the boarding school when we got in.

We stepped off the plane and I smelled the pungent scent of salmon when I put my gray high heels down on the sand. We waited a few minutes, trying to entertain Pat so he wouldn't get fussy, and then I plopped Amy on my hip while we waited for the bus.

The bus finally arrived and I noticed that it had faded yellow paint with some letters missing on the Mount Edgecumbe sign. We climbed aboard and I felt like a fish out of water as we sat next to many of the Natives on their way to their fishing nets. I smelled the salty air from the ocean all over their clothes and felt very out of place with my gray coat on. The people on the bus stared at us and wondered what we were doing there. I also wondered what I was doing there.

After a noisy ride and a few bumpy turns, we arrived at the school where everyone was waiting for us. Again, that blasted coat. I stepped off the bus and saw that all the teachers, who had indeed settled in already, were dressed in jeans and sweatshirts, waiting to greet us. Talk about conspicuous, in more ways than one.

We were already late and had missed the first day of training. We got settled in our dorm rooms with two bunk beds and it was cold. Evidently, the maintenance men didn't turn on the heat during the summer months at Mount Edgecumbe and I was glad that we had packed our warm coats. It rained most of the days we were there and I found out later that Sitka had an annual rainfall of eighty-four inches a year.

After settling in the first day, we met a few teachers from other states in the 'lower forty-eight' who were going through the same thing: culture shock. We became good friends with a couple from Alabama and spent quite a bit of time with them. I loved hearing their Southern accents, as I hadn't been around that many people from the South before. The other couples were from Michigan, Oregon, Washington, Wisconsin, and all points heading north, south, east, or west. It was a diverse group and very few couples had brought small children with them.

We arranged to have one of the wives of a new teacher take care of our children when we went to training with the BIA. We had a few Inupiaq language classes, and since I was a German major in college, I felt I might excel in this area. We didn't learn much in the way of language, however. What I do remember is that we learned how to say, *erasa hactunga* in Inupiaq, or "I have an eraser." We also learned how to say, *alapa*, which means cold . . . a word I would soon say quite often. We also mastered the words *acumlugee* and *nanqlugee* which meant "sit down" and "stand up." In addition, we learned the word for bear, which was *nanuq*. I could use the word bear in the village and I would be able to tell my students to sit down and stand up in their native language. I would also be able to tell them I had an eraser in my hand.

Now, I don't want to be too hard on the instructors for the BIA, as I later found out that the Alaska Native languages had never been written down and were only spread by word of mouth. So, the people training us from the BIA headquarters in Albuquerque, New Mexico, didn't know how to speak many words in the Inupiaq language.

We learned about the history of the Alaska Natives and how much pride they had in their Eskimo ways, such as hunting for caribou, moose, and bear, and fishing for shellfish, whitefish, salmon, and other types of fish which were abundant in the Alaskan waters. In addition, we learned that seal was their main staple and they rendered the fat in a seal poke during the winter. They dipped their dried fish in the seal oil to give it extra flavor.

After they gave us this big spiel about the pride of the Inupiat and Yupik population, I asked the following question of the director of the Bureau of Indian Affairs: "If the Eskimos have so much pride in their culture, why are we flying out to these villages and trying to change their lives?"

The answer from the director was rather terse. He said, "Well, since Alaska became a state in 1959, the Eskimos have quit traveling as nomads and have settled into small villages. The main reason for this is because our government has developed schools there to help the children learn English. Once we started doing this, we can't go back."

I looked at my husband and noticed him shrugging his shoulders. I am sure he thought what I did: if they were okay before we were there, why did we, not knowing anything about their culture, go up there to change their ways? I am not sure I ever got the answer to that question.

We continued with our meetings, then, after a few days, we flew to our own villages. We packed up our small family once more and took the bus to the airport. We flew on a Wien Airlines twin otter toward Kotzebue, Alaska, one of the main hubs for flights across Northern Alaska. As we flew further north, the pilot purposely dropped the nose of the plane toward the ground, giving us a slight bump and a bigger fright. After the jolt, the pilot calmly spoke over the loudspeaker, "You have just crossed the Arctic Circle."

I looked at Rick and our sleeping children, thinking, *where in the world are we?* Yet in some way it was quite exciting and exhilarating. We were part of the Arctic Circle Club.

CHAPTER 16

Becoming a Missionary

We landed in the small airport at Kotzebue, where there was a waiting room made from logs. I noticed that it was quaint. No problems. Then we were supposed to fly out to Selawik, our first assignment, the same day. Now, there were problems. The Bureau of Indian Affairs had hired bush pilots to fly us to Selawik, but being from the 'lower forty-eight' and packing too many personal goods, we couldn't all fit in the small Cessna plane. They had to hire another plane to fly us separately. Rick was in a pink Cessna with Patrick and a few of our boxes. I was assigned to a yellow Cessna and, of course, held little Amy in my arms. Small babies always stay with their mothers. I didn't like the idea of flying without Rick and Pat, but we didn't have a choice.

We loaded up in each of our small planes and were off. Our flight took at least one hour, as Selawik was ninety miles from Kotzebue, and I was a little frightened as I climbed into the yellow Cessna. I had never flown in such a tiny plane before, and we were in Alaska after all. I had no idea what was going to happen, and I had my baby along.

As we were flying, I looked down at the sights below. All the way to Selawik, all I could see was flat land with intermittent puddles of water, pools of water, and larger spots of water. There were miles and miles of jagged lakes with bits of land between. It looked like a large puzzle. The pilot was flying fairly low to the ground, but besides the tundra, I saw nothing. No man or animal. I couldn't believe it. Was this where we were going to live for a whole year?

The pilot could see the consternation in my face and knew what I was thinking. He quietly said, "You'll get used to it. There isn't much out here all right, but the people are very nice. We'll be in Selawik soon and you'll see the village on either side of the river."

Finally, the pilot took a large swoop over the village and yelled, "There it is, that's Selawik."

What did he say? That was Selawik. Where in the world was I going to be living? Ninety miles from nowhere, by plane only, and where was the village? As I mentioned earlier, all I could see were dots of something. Then he told me to look out the window, where I would see the Selawik River rising up to greet us. He also told me that we would be landing on a gravel runway . . . a gravel runway? How did that work?

I didn't have time to change my mind. Bump! Bump! We were down. I was at the mercy of the pilot and I didn't know what to expect. The people in the village had been alerted that their new teachers were arriving on this day, so there were many villagers lining both sides of the runway. As Amy and I were escorted down the small plane steps by our bush pilot, the people rushed up to greet us. I saw brown, tanned faces and coal black hair covering all of their heads. Again, I felt conspicuous. At least I wasn't wearing my gray suede coat. I had learned that about the bush already. The tundra wasn't meant for fashion; at least not the kind from the 'lower forty-eight.' Clothing on the tundra was meant for survival, warmth, and comfort. No high heels here.

What would they think of us? I remember wondering if this was how people from diverse cultures felt when they walked into a room where most of the people present are from a different culture. It was disconcerting, but a lesson well learned.

Feeling ill at ease, I told the pilot I would like to wait until Rick flew in with Pat to cross the river to the other side of the village. That was where the school and our quarters were. He radioed the other pilot and told me that Rick and Pat were arriving soon in their pink Cessna.

I waited, shaking hands and smiling at the children and adults standing by. I thought I was in a foreign land.

Rick finally arrived and climbed out of the pink Cessna, helping Pat crawl down on his own. He was almost two by then and was getting heavy to carry, especially down the small metal steps. Rick smiled at me as he got off the plane, looking a little piqued. I don't know if it was from being sick from the plane ride or sick from realizing where we were going to be for a year. I thought that maybe he would apologize to me for getting me into this. No such luck.

Some of the people in the village had brought their boats to the river so they could take us over to the school and our quarters. We climbed in the rowboats, or skiffs, as they call them in Alaska, and headed downstream to Selawik. There was a beautiful little girl in my boat who had shiny blue-black hair going all the way down her back. I wasn't sure if she could speak English or not. I asked her how she got around in the village, and I will always remember what she said, "Me, I run like rabbit."

Her English name was Millie, and I found out she was in the fourth grade. Millie, this darling girl with the big smile and broken accented English, was going to be my student. How lucky I was to be with such an enthusiastic little girl.

As we were winding our way down the river toward the village, I thought about the pioneers I read about in grade school back in Plaza, and how I was also a pioneer to be teaching in an Eskimo village in

1968. It was only nine years after Alaska had become a state. I was feeling quite full of myself, picturing how I was going to be another Margaret Mead teaching the people all the ways of the world . . . a missionary of sorts.

What happened to me next cured me of that notion. We arrived at the shore across the river from the airport where there were young men and boys standing on the bank of the river. They began helping us out of the skiffs and carried our boxes to our new quarters. I noticed that many of the children had the odor of fish hanging over them. Since it was still summer, the men were dressed in blue jeans and they wore brown canvas jackets. Others wore flannel shirts, and the girls wore skirts and blouses with their hair tied back in colorful handkerchiefs that matched their skirts, which led me to believe that their mothers knew how to sew. Most of the adults and children wore black rubber boots that had been purchased from the 'lower forty-eight because it was still muddy in the village from the winter thaw.

Boys from the ages of nine to twelve carried our goods to the quarters. Many children were wanting to visit us the minute we got in the door. First, I had to digest that the building looked like h old military quarters, with white painted wood slats and a tall set of painted steps; nothing like the home I was going to buy one day. But, we had heat from a furnace and electricity; something I later found out that the people in the village did not have. How could I be so ungrateful?

As I mentioned earlier, several children kept knocking on our door. When I opened it, they would say, "Visit?"

I didn't know what to do, and being the polite person I thought I was, I would let them in. The children were between seven and ten years old. They would come in, sit down on our beige Naugahyde furniture, and stay and stay and stay . . . I really didn't know how to get them to leave. It seemed that they hadn't been taught the same kind of manners we had in the lower forty-eight, where we were taught that you don't go to someone's house without being invited, and you don't overstay your welcome. These old sayings were the farthest thing from their minds. They were curious about their new teachers and the babies that came with them. The children offered to pick up Amy and carry her around with no hesitation. It seemed that they were very familiar with tiny children and they felt very comfortable in that position. When Amy started to cry, they would take her over to the window and tap on it, distracting her from her tears . . . and it worked. I soon picked up their wonderful example of keeping a child's attention on something else when they became fussy.

One morning, when we were still unpacking our goods, I received another knock at the door. I opened it and there were four cherub-looking children facing me. Instead of the typical blonde locks as seen in many of Raphael's paintings, these children had dark cropped hair shaped in little bowls around their cheeks. They were adorable. I asked one of the boys what his name was, and he replied, "Nanuq." I was elated that I knew what his name meant in Inupiaq and replied, "Oh, Nanuq! Your name means bear in your language."

He looked at me with one eye cocked and said, "What? No, my name is Leonard. Leonard Brown."

I could have sworn that he told me his name was Nanuq. Did I feel like a fool! With red cheeks, I just said, "Oh, I'm sorry. I thought you said your name was Nanuq."

The children laughed hysterically, then they handed me a white bowl. I held on to it for a minute and looked inside. It was full of dark berries they had picked from the tundra that morning. I thought they were giving them to me as a gift for *their new teacher*. Then one of the children looked at me with a puzzled look, and said, "That will be a dollar please."

So much for knowing the Inupiaq language and being a missionary. I had a lot to learn.

As a side note, if you are wondering why the Alaska Natives had English names instead of their Inupiat or Yupik names, it is because missionaries often renamed Native Alaskans with Christian names or English names.

CHAPTER 17

Reality Sets In

Here we were on the tundra with two little children and an apartment to live in that looked like part of a military barrack. I did not mind the apartment, but I had a hard time getting used to cooking on an old cook stove that had been converted to a gas stove. I could barely pick up the grates to check on the source because they were so heavy. At least when the stove was on, the kitchen was warm. I had to boil our water and set it outside my kitchen window to cool it before we drank it. I remember thinking, *I can't even go to a faucet and get a drink of water.*

The lowest temperature we had in Selawik was forty degrees below zero with a ten-mile-an-hour wind. We bought special parkas and pants made from goose feathers in Seattle before we flew to Selawik which took away the cold, but in forty below, the air still stung our knees.

What saved us that year was having a wonderful maintenance man named Leonard Davis and a caring babysitter in his wife, Helen Davis. Leonard had served in the military, so he knew how to speak English and he made us feel 'at home' in Selawik.

Based on movies I had seen in the lower forty-eight, I asked Leonard, "Do Eskimos really rub noses to kiss?"

He replied, "Me, I kiss them right on the mouth."

Leonard kept the generators running, and he and Helen took our family on a boat ride where we had a picnic near the Selawik river. Helen made homemade bread while I was teaching and carried my baby Amy on her back while she was working around the house. Her little girl, Beverly, played outside with Patrick, and I remember them using a broken rocking chair and sledding outside our quarters.

My teaching load was large, as I had thirty-four students in grades one and two all in one classroom. Fortunately, the Inupiat children were very well behaved and I also had a teacher's aide who helped me in the classroom. Her name was Jean Jacobs and she spoke English and Inupiat. She often translated for me when I visited the elderly in the village. She had gone to a boarding school called Chemawa Indian School near Salem, Oregon, for her high school years, so she knew our culture more than other people in the village. She was invaluable to me as a teacher's aide and as a friend. Jean also helped me enjoy myself in the village and took me to meet some of her friends. She also told me old folk tales about the Inupiat culture, and I was fascinated. For instance, I saw an elderly Inupiat woman who had speckled arms. Jean told me that the legend says that her arms were speckled because her mother mated with a salmon.

After one year at Selawik, we fell in love with the students and the adults in the village and realized that we wanted to stay another year. So much for the new house in Bellingham; it was the furthest thing from our minds. Teaching in Alaska was fun and exciting.

Close Friendship between Patrick Gilmore and Beverly Davis

CHAPTER 18

No New House

After teaching one more year in Selawik, we decided to stay another year in Alaska because we were enjoying ourselves so much. We called Bethel to tell them we would like to teach in another village and we were told that all the villages were taken. Then Mr. Benson paused and said, "I see there is one village that has not been filled, and it is Nightmute, Alaska."

"What is it like, Mr. Benson?" Rick asked over the two way radio.

"Well, it is a Yupik village and it is very small. It has only one hundred people and you and Deanna will be the only teachers there. Most of the people there speak only Yupik."

I overheard this conversation and I thought, *Oh no, I have to learn a new language after learning some Inupiat. I will have to start all over..*

"We'll take it!" I heard my husband say into the speaker.

He got off the radio and I looked at him. "So now what do we do?"

Rick answered, "We'll pack our things and go back to Bellingham for the summer and stay in the dorms. You and I can take classes and enjoy ourselves in the lower forty-eight before we fly back up to

Nightmute in August. We can see if we can get your niece to babysit while we go to school at Western."

That is exactly what we did. My niece, Karen, was invaluable, as she stayed with our two children while we attended classes. We were also able to visit Mr. and Mrs. Born and Maureen Darting and her family for those few summer months. When it is not raining, Bellingham, Washington, is a beautiful place to live.

After spending the summer in Bellingham, going to school, eating out in restaurants, and going to movies, it was time to return to our new village. Nightmute was located on the Kuskokwim River about ninety miles from Bethel, Alaska. We had to take a float plane, as there were no runways in Nightmute. In the summer, the people flew in and out of the village on float planes, and when the river was frozen, the planes used skis to land. There were around one hundred residents in this village, and only ten or so could speak English: the school cook, the health aide, the maintenance man, and one of the men in the village who married a Yupik lady. Some of the students could speak English because they learned it in school.

Since the people of Nightmute had only had a school for a few years before we arrived, they were very curious about us. In fact, one day I heard a knock on the door and I opened it. An elderly Yupik woman with long, stringy black hair and ivory earrings stepped in and followed me to the kitchen without saying a word. She couldn't speak English, so she just sat down on the linoleum floor and stared at me. She was wearing a lady's gusspaq or parka and mukluks. I smiled and didn't know what to do, so I decided to offer her some tea. Based on my prior experience of teaching in Selawik for two years, I knew that most Alaska natives liked to drink hot tea. They often drank it while eating dried herring dipped in seal oil. She nodded, "Yes," when I indicated by my gestures that I was offering her some tea.

She stayed on the floor for about twenty-five minutes and watched me wash dishes and work in the kitchen. Then she got up and left the house.

That was my introduction to where I was going to be living for the coming year. I also had a jolt when I realized that the teacher's aide who normally worked with the teachers and interpreted for them was going to be gone for the first week of school. Funerals are very important to Alaska Natives, and they take precedence over any job a person might have. It is part of their culture.

So, the first day of school, I walked into the multi-level class of sixteen students and said, "Hello. My name is Mrs. Gilmore and I am going to be your teacher. Can you tell me your names?"

All sixteen students just stared at me with blank faces and did not say a thing. I didn't really know what to do, so I stepped outside the door and said a silent prayer to God and begged Him to help me. I walked back in and tried again. "Does anyone in this room speak any English?"

One of the older girls with light-colored pigtails slowly raised her hand. "I do," she said.

Her name was Anna Doll, and it was her father who spoke English because his father was a Norwegian fisherman who had settled in the village of Nightmute a long time ago. I didn't care where she came from. She saved my life that day, and for the rest of the week, she was my interpreter and helper. I would say something in English to the students and she would tell the little ones what I just said in Yupik. We managed the rest of the week without Joseph Fairburn, my adult teacher's aide. Anna was one of my top students the rest of the year; and when Joseph came back, he became a good friend and great teacher's aide.

There was no TV, no radio, and not a lot to do in that tiny town. I had to think of things to fill my time so I wouldn't go stir crazy, or "bushy," as they say in Alaska.

While teaching in the lower forty-eight for a few years before going to Alaska, I had learned how to play square ball on the playground.

I was first introduced to the game while teaching second grade in Westminster, California. Then, I participated in this form of recreation when I taught fourth grade near Bellingham, Washington. I thought it was a wonderful game, and when I was on recess duty, I didn't just watch, I played with the kids.

Now, what can you do in Nightmute, Alaska, when it was blowing snow and thirty degrees below zero during most of the winter months? Play square ball, of course! I moved the desks and chairs aside during the nighttime hours and used masking tape to make the four squares we needed to complete the picture. The Bureau of Indian Affairs furnished us with the rubber balls we needed for the game, so I kept a special stash in my coat cupboard for nights like this. The children of all ages came up to the school when they saw the lights on after dark, which happened around 4:00 p.m. in the winter months.

It was on one of these freezing nights that I decided to go over to the school and play square ball. This time, there were only a few students brave enough to come up through the blizzard to play, but about ten of them did. Patrick was also there by my side and tried to join in when he had his turn. The older children were patient with him, as he was so young and often missed the ball.

Next to my classroom was the guest room. The room was used for lodging when we had people come up from the lower forty-eight to minister to the Yupik people. They might be from Fish and Wildlife, Social Services, or other government agencies. We had to cook for them and they stayed in the small room with the bunk beds.

During one cold night while we were playing, some of my fourth grade students were in the hall waiting their turn to play. They came to me and said, "Mrs. Gilmore, there is someone in the guest room. We can hear their feet and some noise."

I said, "There can't be. There is no one staying in the guest room tonight."

Paul John, a little boy with a round face and a big dimple replied, "But Mrs. Gilmore, we can hear them inside."

I was bewildered and stopped the game. I knew I was going to put an end to these shenanigans. I marched right over to the locked door, heard feet shuffling, and shook the handle, saying rather loudly, "You kids get out of there. You are not supposed to be in the guest room."

I figured they might have climbed through the window and were just messing around inside. No one answered, so I shook the handle on the door once again, "I said, you need to come out of there."

This time, there wasn't a sound, but the handle shook back at me. Now, I was getting a little frightened. I told my son Patrick to go to the house and get the keys to the guest room from his dad and bring them back to me. Luckily, the wind had died down and he was able to go up the wooden steps to our quarters and get the key from his dad.

Pat came back with the key, and all the children were huddled around me waiting to see the people inside. They could see by my face that I was pretty worried. I took the keys from Pat and slowly put them in the lock. I opened the door and expected to see some children or mischievous adults inside. I walked in and no one was in the room.

I thought that they must have climbed out the window before I got there, so I went over to the windowsill. To my great surprise, I noticed that the latch to the window was closed from the inside and there was no way anyone could shut it from the outside. My only explanation was that we must have been visited by a ghost. I was quite perplexed, and some of the older students suggested that we bring one of the elders up from the village to sprinkle holy water in the hall and the surrounding area. The village people were predominantly Catholic, and I, being of the same denomination, thought this might be a wise thing to do. Two of the older students ran down the long wooden steps, and after a long wait, one of the older men in the village came up with some holy water. He was one of the deacons at the church, so he said a few prayers, sprinkled the holy water in the guest room, and returned home.

We stopped playing square ball and went home for the evening. To this day, my family and I talk about this incident, but we really don't have a good explanation for what happened there. We have discovered in the interim that Nightmute is known to have the third highest ghost sightings in Alaska.

One other eventful thing happened while we were teaching in Nightmute. It was a school day and I woke up as usual. Then, when I undid my covers, I noticed that when I was breathing, pockets of air floated ahead of me. The heat was off and it was twenty-two degrees below zero inside our house. Luckily, the whole family was covered in down blankets for the night, so we hadn't noticed it go off. I looked in our bird cage and our little turquoise parakeet had frozen during the night. I didn't want the children to see that, so I bundled them up and we headed for the school where we still had some heat. The copper pipes in our house were frozen.

Rick went down to the village to get the maintenance man and asked him to come up to help us. Tony Henry immediately obliged, and when he arrived, Rick went into the living room to call Bethel to ask them what we should do.

Mr. Benson told Rick, "Whatever you do, don't light the oil stove or it might blow up."

While he was on the phone with Mr. Benson, Rick heard a loud explosion and he went to the kitchen. There was Tony Henry, lying flat out on the floor, and the grate from the stove was way across the room. When Tony came to after the blast, he slowly stood up and was covered in black soot. All you could see were the whites of his eyes. Rick checked him over to see if he was all right. Since they both realized he was okay, they just looked at each other and started laughing.

Tony said, "I think there was hair in the line."

Rick asked, "Hair in the line?"

"Yes, you know, hair in the line."

Rick realized that he meant there was air in the line and they both continued to chuckle.

Tony Henry thawed out the pipes during the day and we were able to return to our warm home after school that evening.

Finally, spring came to Nightmute, and I decided to go for a walk down to the village. It was good to get out after the long winter, even if I couldn't visit with the locals. Nightmute, like most of the villages located on the tundra, had boardwalks. It was too hard to walk on the soggy wet dirt because there were many bumps and creases.

As I was walking that morning, my rubber boots slipped on a patch of ice and I fell off the boardwalk. I fell directly into a puddle of water, and when I stood up, my parka was all covered with mud. I was embarrassed, but I looked all around and I didn't see anyone, so I climbed back on the boardwalk and ran back to my home. No one had seen me fall . . . or so I thought.

It was time to celebrate the seal hunting season, so the villagers had a special dance in the dance hall. I attended with my children, Patrick and Amy, because I wanted them to have this special cultural experience. As the night went on, the ladies in the village got up to do a special dance. In it, they depicted a lady walking and then falling off a boardwalk, where they all grabbed their back and said, "Ugh" in a loud manner. Everyone laughed very hard and I realized they were telling my story. Evidently, someone had seen me fall after all. They invited me to come join them in the dance, and of course I did. I laughed every time I performed it as well.

At times, women want to talk to other women about their children, husbands, vacation, visiting others, etc. I could not do that. The women in the village would not understand me since I spoke broken Yupik at best. I told Rick to ask our boss, Mr. Benson, if we could move to Tununak the next year. Tununak had a resident priest who lived there and a lady volunteer from the lower forty-eight who ran a Montessori school in the village, and if we lived there I would be able to visit with them now and then. Understanding our request, Mr. Benson assigned us to teach in Tununak, Alaska, the following year.

NIGHTMUTE SCHOOL AND RICK AND DEANNA WEARING MUSKRAT PARKAS

CHAPTER 19

The Gem of the North

Tununak, Alaska, was a beautiful village located on Nelson Island. On one side was the Kuskokwim River and on the other side it bordered the Bering Sea. The school and our home were located on a hill overlooking the village. When the sun was shining, whether it was in the winter with ten feet of snow on the ground or the spring when the ice was melting in the Kuskokwim, Tununak was heavenly.

Our home was new and it looked like an apartment in the lower forty-eight. The furniture was modern and our kitchen and bathroom had all new appliances. We had running water and electricity while the people in the village did not. I always felt a little embarrassed by what we were given compared to the villagers. The Alaskan tundra presented problems related to giving everyone plumbing and water resources at the time. I tried to share what we had with the villagers, and my daughter would often bring her friends to take a shower with our running water. The girls would stay in there for an hour or so, just splashing and having a good time.

The school was attached to the apartments, and Rick and I were the only teachers for the first year. I was four months pregnant with my third child when we arrived in Tununak, and I was thrilled at the prospect of having another baby. I felt the butterfly kicks that come with the second trimester.

Then, one night, I felt the pangs of labor, and I told Rick, "I think I am going to have this baby."

"You can't, Deanna. You are not far enough along."

"I know that, but I think I am having a miscarriage."

It was the middle of the night and the pains got worse. I had previously talked to the women in the village about having babies without doctors, and they said they just knelt down and the baby came out.

I thought I might have to do that as well. I did not wake up Rick and took a clean sheet and spread it on the bathroom floor. I knelt down and the baby came out. I was pretty upset and the umbilical cord was still on the baby, so I just pulled it out. Needless to say, I started hemorrhaging and I told Rick to contact the village health aide. Rick walked down to the aide's house and told him to come see me.

The aide was excellent and had been trained well. He radioed the doctor in Bethel and told him to send out a twin otter to pick me up and take me to the hospital.

In about an hour, the plane arrived, and by that time I had lost a lot of blood. The pilot and a male nurse had me lie down on a metal cot on the floor of the plane and we took off for Bethel. Since I had hemorrhaged a lot, the male nurse tried to get an IV drip in my arm but he couldn't find any veins that worked. I think he poked me about ten times before he found a vein that had blood in it. I arrived at the hospital and the doctor gave me some blood transfusions. I stayed in the hospital until they knew I was well enough to return to the village. It was a close call, but God wasn't ready to take me home.

I returned to the village and mourned the loss of my baby girl, who I named Heather.

The priest who lived there comforted me as well when I returned, and the teacher aides ran the class for a couple of days before I returned to teaching.

That Christmas, I had my students perform a play in Yupik just as I had in Nightmute the year before. After the play was over, a little girl brought Amy to me, and Amy, who was four years old then, was as white as a sheet. I asked the girl "What is wrong with Amy?"

The older girl with her said, "It's all right Mrs. Gilmore. Just give her some ice-cold water. She chewed too much Copenhagen."

I realized then that Amy had become 'one of the gang,' so to speak, and there wasn't much I could do about it. I wanted her to play with the other children, and it was normal for the mothers to give their children some Copenhagen after they had chewed it. To be nice, the children shared it with their friend, Amy . . .

After giving her an ice-cold glass of water, she indeed came out of her funk and continued to play with her friend. I told Rick what had happened and we continued on with our lives.

We returned to the lower forty-eight to attend summer school in Bellingham, and my beloved niece Karen came with us once again. We enjoyed being able to go to stores to shop and eat at restaurants. Rick and I also liked the classes we were taking at Western Washington University, and I started working on my master's degree in education administration.

There were twenty-two people in my class who were studying to be principals or school superintendents. This was in 1972, and I was the only woman in the class. Normally, after being deprived of male companionship during my high school years, I would enjoy the attention from men. But instead, I felt a little out of place. Were there no other women who wanted to become principals or superintendents during these years?

When we returned to the village of Tununak for the next year, I discovered that I was pregnant once again. I was delighted that this had happened, and the best part was that the baby would be born in the summer, so I could stay home and take care of him or her.

The second year we were in Tununak, the BIA hired another teacher to join us, as our class loads were remarkably high. Jean Thompson came late in the fall to relieve us of our heavy load. The children all ran up to the school to tell me when she arrived and yelled, "skuldukta, skuldukta," the Yupik name for schoolteacher.

I asked them, "What does the new skuldukta look like?"

I was hoping that she would be an older lady so I would not have to compete for attention from my husband. After all, she would be living right down the hall from us and the nights were long.

The children said, "She has white hair and she is big."

Oh, good, I thought to myself. *She is an older lady and is kind of plump.*

As the school principal, Rick went down to help her up to the school. Some of the men from the village also brought in some of her luggage. The first thing I noticed was that she had a metal trunk with stars and stripes all over it . . . not luggage an older woman would carry. Then I saw her. She had white hair all right; as in long, blonde, flowing locks. She was about twenty-eight years old and looked like the movie star Lonnie Anderson. Rick looked at me and shrugged his shoulders as if to say, "I didn't order this."

I brought Jean Thompson in for tea and we hit it off right away. I found out that she was also a Catholic and had the same birthday as I did. How could it go wrong? She was a terrific teacher and my son was in her class. We did many things together and she was good company for me, Rick, and our entire family.

CHAPTER 20

It Was Not Enough for Me

At the end of our fifth year of teaching in Alaska, I told Rick that I would like to move back to Bellingham, Washington, so I could have our baby in a hospital and not risk having a miscarriage in the bush again. He understood my feelings and we decided to go back to the lower forty-eight so I would feel comfortable having my baby there. We put in our resignation papers with great hopes of new adventures, and I was finally going to live in my dream home.

And a gorgeous home it was. We found a split-level home in Lynden, Washington, which was about fourteen miles from Bellingham. It had a circular driveway surrounded by fourteen-feet-tall fir trees. It also had a fountain in the middle of the island, and it was heaven.

We arrived during the summer, and this time Karen did not come along. I was going to be the perfect mother, and I did not need a babysitter nor did I go to school. I was nine months pregnant, and while Pat and Amy enjoyed playing outside in the heat, I stayed inside and tried to remain comfortable.

Rick was worried about getting a job, and I was waiting to have a baby. I was due on July 10, but nothing happened. By the twentieth of

July, I asked my primary doctor if he could induce me since I was getting quite uncomfortable. He agreed, and I went to Saint Joseph's Hospital, where he began the procedure. In the middle of my contractions, which were strong and steady, I wished I had waited for this baby to come out when he or she wanted to. Finally, after a painful delivery, our beautiful little girl was born and she was very healthy. I thanked God for that, and we named her Tara Lynn. I remember Rick saying that he was excited for another girl so he could take her to get a milkshake one day.

I spent the rest of the summer in a blissful state, as I was able to nurse Tara with no complications, and in August, we enrolled Pat and Amy in the public school in Lynden, where Pat was in the second grade and Amy was in kindergarten. They both liked their teachers, so that was wonderful. Every school day, I made fresh chocolate chip cookies and had them waiting on the counter when they got off the bus.

Rick was hired as a director of a school for mentally disabled adults in Bellingham, Washington, so he wasn't worried about providing for our family. He enjoyed his job, and each day, I vacuumed the living room, made the beds, and washed and folded the towels and clothes and waited . . . I waited for the kids to come home at 3:00 p.m., and then I watched the clock to see when it would 5:00 p.m., which was when my husband got home from work. Every day I waited! I spent many hours playing with my darling baby and tried to be 'Holly Homemaker.'

But it wasn't enough for me. I was very bored and I became depressed. You see, I had spent five years teaching wonderful children in the Alaskan bush, and I had fallen in love with my students in every village. With their large brown, penetrating eyes and their broad, innocent smiles, they had captured my heart, body, and soul.

I dreamt about certain students and missed them very much. One of them was a little girl named Margaret Cooper, who had the spirit of an untamed colt. She visited me often in our teacher's quarters and was always game to go on an adventure. I remember when we climbed the high rocks behind our house with other children and walked along the beach near the Bering Sea collecting rocks. I can still see her smile to this day.

After one year of living in my dream home, I asked Rick to sit down when he got home from work.

"Rick, I want to go back to Alaska to teach again. I am not happy being a homemaker. It's just not enough for me."

Rick said, "I thought you wanted to come back to the lower forty-eight and be the perfect mother to our kids."

With tears in my eyes, I replied, "Women who like being homemakers are fulfilled keeping their houses clean and tending to the children, and I admire them for their work. I just cannot do it. I want to teach."

Rick answered, "Well, I've been thinking the same thing for a while. There is a lot of stress at my job because I have to make speeches at the United Way, Elk's Club, and other places to ask for donations. This is so I can pay the employees, and it is a worry to me. Maybe we should go back to teach for the BIA, as we will have a steady income and you will get to teach your students again."

After weighing the pros and cons, he made the call.

We were accepted right away, as it takes a certain kind of person to live in the bush and we had proven ourselves already. As it happened, we did go back for three more years, but it was never the same. That is always the way, isn't it? When you try to duplicate a wonderful experience, it doesn't always happen.

We were sent to a new village on the Kuskokwim River called Kwethluk. We were supporting teachers. Rick had been the principal in two of our villages, so it was hard for him not to be the leader. There were three sets of teachers, but for some reason, we did not hit it off with the principal and his wife. This had never happened in the other villages, especially the ones where we were the only teachers or had one extra teacher. After a year of teaching there, we asked to be moved to another village.

Mr. Benson assigned us to a large village called Emmonak located on the Yukon River. The village had 600 people, so the school had many students. Rick was assigned as the principal, and three other couples taught with us. Two of the couples were younger than us, and I remember that the male teacher had sixteen brothers and sisters in his family. He said that they could have their own baseball game within their own family. The other couple had a baby girl, and one of the couples were older than us. All three couples were new to the bush, so they relied on us to show them the ropes. We got along very well with the other teachers and had a great year there.

While we were in Emmonak, the Bureau of Indian Affairs called my husband on the two-way radio and asked him if we would like to start a band there. Someone had donated brand new instruments to the school and it would be wonderful if someone could teach the kids how to use them. Rick knew me and thought I might like the challenge, so he said, "Yes! Send them out on the plane and I will have Deanna teach them how to be in a band."

Remember, I learned how to play the saxophone in Plaza and I played the piano by ear. I knew if I could get hold of the instruments ahead of time, I could learn to play them well enough to teach beginning band in Emmonak, and that is just what I did.

The instruments arrived before school started, so I opened each case like they were immaculate treasures and polished them with the cloth that came with them. I ordered some beginning band books and extra reeds for the woodwinds. I took them to our quarters and learned how to play each one. Granted, I was better on the saxophone and the clarinet, as I had played the saxophone in my Plaza days, and I tackled the trumpet and trombone with some ease. I was not good on the flute, as I couldn't quite get the correct lip placement for the instrument.

When the students returned to school that fall, I had the children in grades five to eight sign up for band and tell me which instrument they would like to play. They had never been in a band, but they had seen and heard people play the instruments in movies. The village elders ordered movies from the lower forty-eight and showed them at the community hall to fill some time during the long, frigid winters.

The first day of band practice, I passed out the cases with their instruments in them. I tried to give each student their first choice, but I could not always grant them their wishes. When they opened up the cases, their eyes got wide and they had large grins on their faces. They were proud to hold the instruments in their hands.

I took each section and asked the other students to be quiet as I showed each group how to assemble their instruments. This was an after-school activity, so it did not matter how long it took us to do this.

We practiced every night after school with twenty-one members of the band. We learned how to play "Go Tell Aunt Rhodie," "Mary Had a Little Lamb," "Three Blind Mice," and "Twinkle, Twinkle Little Star." Good bands always have a concert for the parents and relatives, so that November, I placed fall leaves on a curtain in the community hall and we played the four songs we had learned. They did very well, and the people in Emmonak were so proud of the students who performed in the band. They gave me a round of applause, as well.

Deanna leads a band in Emmonak, Alaska

CHAPTER 21

Special Gift in Emmonak

Something must have been in the water, or it might have been the dark winter, because I found out I was pregnant again with our fourth baby. I knew all the symptoms, and since we did not have a doctor to talk to, I discussed my possible due date with the local health aide. Based on both of our calculations, she estimated that the baby would be due in May of 1976 . . . Rick and I were both delighted, but we did not tell anyone until I started to show that I was pregnant. We had done this once before when we lost a child, so we wanted to be sure.

Besides starting a band and teaching fourth grade, I was the girl's junior high basketball coach. I had played basketball on the girl's team at Holy Names Academy, so I figured I could handle this job, as well.

We had a pretty good team, as we had a set of eighth-grade twins that were quite tall for their age, and they weren't afraid to get a little tough. We even got to fly to another village to play for the junior high championship game for the BIA schools and we were victorious.

When Christmas rolled around, I directed a play for the older students, who performed it in Yupik. I had my teacher's aide translate the words from English to Yupik. The other teachers did their part as well, and had their students perform plays and sing songs. The entire village attended the program because this was where the families exchanged their Christmas presents. One of the village elders dressed up like Santa Claus and passed out presents to the children. Each family passed out their own presents after Santa Claus left the building.

Since this was such a large village, the whole program lasted for four long hours, but what else did we have to do when it was twenty below zero on December 24, 1976? Emmonak happened to be a Catholic village, so we attended Mass on Christmas day and sang some Yupik and English Christmas carols. After a short vacation where we played games with our children and ate meals with our friends from the village, we returned to school.

I had the band stay after school again and we worked on harder pieces. We were getting ready for our spring concert. On March 19, I decorated some drapes in the community hall with crepe paper roses and flowers. That night we held our spring concert and played some harder pieces than "Three Blind Mice," but I can only remember playing "Oh, Susanna." Perhaps that is because as I was tossing my baton to conduct the band, I felt sharp pains in my lower abdomen. I finished the concert, asked one of the older students to put down the chairs and music stands, and told him that I wasn't feeling well.

Rick and the children were already home by the time I trudged through the heavy storm door of our quarters. As I walked in, I looked at Rick with a little fear and told him, "I think I am in labor, Rick."

"You can't be. The baby isn't due until May."

"I know, but I think it is coming early. Maybe you should go get Bart Donigan to fly me out to Bethel, then I can fly down to Anchorage so I can have the baby in a hospital with a doctor on hand."

"I'll go right away and get him," Rick said.

Rick put on his heavy parka and walked out into the deep snow as flakes started falling all around him.

It was only March 21, and the baby was supposed to be born in May. Was I going to lose another one of my children to the tundra?

The labor pains continued while I waited for Rick to return from talking to Bart. Finally, he walked through my bedroom door with a sad expression on his face, "Deanna, Bart can't take you because it is snowing too hard and we are going to have a storm. He can't fly in this weather. He told me that his wife Sharon might help, as she was a nurse and delivered some babies before. That is all we can do at this point."

Anyone who has lived in Alaska knows that you do not fly a small plane when there is low visibility, so Sharon Donigan put on her parka and left for our house right away.

In the meantime, I told Rick to find an empty shoebox in the closet, put a blanket in it, and set it on the warming shelf above the stove in case we need to keep the baby warm before help arrived.

It was late by then, and my own children had gone to bed because Pat and Amy had school in the morning. Tara was asleep in her crib in the room next to ours.

I was in labor the whole night, with Rick and Sharon by my side. Although Sharon was a missionary, I didn't care and let out a few cuss words when the pains got unbearable. The school health aide also came early in the morning to assist, and she said to Rick, "Boil some water, please, Mr. Gilmore."

Rick had watched scenes like this in the movies so he got pretty nervous as he placed the metal teapot on the stove. The health aide saw that his hand was shaking as he poured the water into the teapot and she chuckled, "Mr. Gilmore, why are you so nervous? I just want a cup of tea."

That kind of broke the ice for him as I was in the bedroom about to give birth.

Prior to this, Rick had never witnessed the birth of one of our children. When our other three were born, it was during the time when fathers were escorted out of the delivery room to wait on an empty chair while his child was born.

Around 6:00 in the morning, Sharon said, "The baby is almost out now. Give it one last push."

I did as she said while Rick held my hand and out came the baby. Sharon caught the baby in her hands and held him up. "It's a boy and he is healthy!"

She proceeded to cut the umbilical cord and waited for the placenta to expel, which it did with ease.

I did not know it at the time, but since school was out for the day, the other teachers had been seated in our living room the whole time I gave birth. I'm glad I kept from swearing during the actual birth, as I might have been embarrassed by my language.

It was the easiest birth I had, as he was only six pounds, eight ounces, a big contrast to Patrick, who had been nine pounds, six ounces and had to be pulled out of me. I was in a state of euphoria and even got up to get my own cup of tea and greet our visitors. Patrick came in to see the baby and he had a big grin on his face. He had a little brother. We named him Brian Christopher, and our calculations must have been off because he was extremely healthy, active, and a joy to have as a member of our family. He was our special gift born in Emmonak, Alaska.

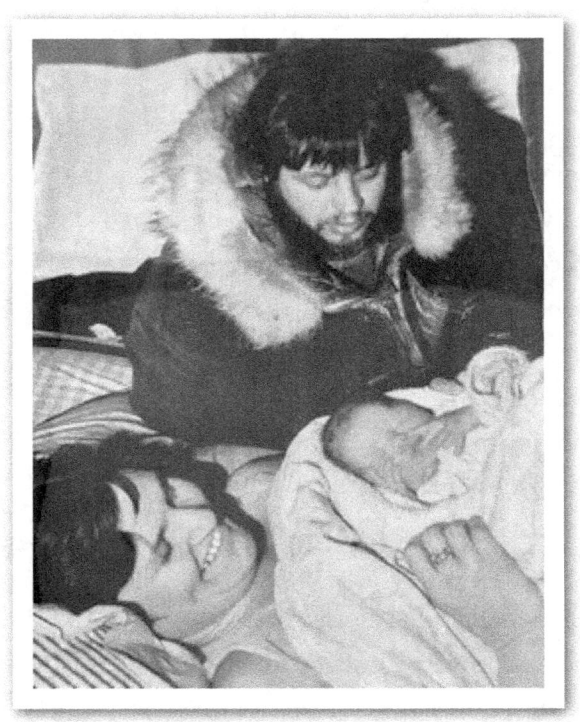

A Special Gift in Emmonak

CHAPTER 22

Our Last Hurrah

The State of Alaska decided to take over the BIA school in Emmonak the same year I started the band. In fact, at the end of the year, we had to pack all of the instruments up and send them back to our headquarters in Bethel, Alaska. It was a hard time for us, as we enjoyed the village very much and I was sad about the students losing their band experience. But we had no choice in the matter, so we called Mr. Benson and asked him where he would be sending us next. He told us that there was a BIA school open in Quinhagak, Alaska. It was still in the Bethel region, and it was close to a larger town called Dillingham. We decided to take it, as that was our only option.

Quinhagak was the first village we had seen that had an actual road. It was gravel and it went for about a mile and then back to the village. The maintenance man's name was Martin Friend, and he lived up to his moniker. He was friendly and very helpful. He also had a truck and he let us ride in it back and forth on the one-mile road. We thought we were really living.

Our babysitter was an older lady with a wonderful smile, and she welcomed our family with open arms. By then, we had all four of our children. Pat and Amy attended school while Charity Morgan took care of our two little ones, Tara, who was at that point three years old, and Brian, who was five months old. Charity packed him inside her parka on her back when she worked around the house. Rick was the principal, and we had two supporting teachers who were from the South in the United States. They were a wonderful couple and they had two darling red-headed children. We spent our holidays together as well as our teaching days at the school.

Quinhagak was a Moravian village, and the only time we attended church there was for a funeral. A young girl that Rick taught got hepatitis and died while we were there. It was pretty scary, because Rick was her teacher and we thought he might get it since it was the contagious kind, and sure enough, he came down with it. I got it from him and became quite ill. We both took days off school while the teachers' aides covered our classes. It was painful and the whites of our eyes became yellow. Hepatitis is hard to recover from and it took us several months to return to our original health.

Eventually, we both became well again and returned to our teaching duties. Patrick was in the fifth grade and often played basketball with the young boys from the village. Through no fault of their own, the children sometimes gave white kids a hard time. This feeling had been developing over time as our government imposed more rules for the Alaska Native people to follow. The rules were not always logical. As an example, the Department of Fish and Game set a limit on the amount of ducks the Alaska Natives could shoot. For years, they had been killing as many ducks as they wanted because they used them for food and subsistence living. That was not the only thing that created resistance to the white man's ways, but that list is too long to go into for this missive. Suffice it to say that even unwarranted prejudice existed. Patrick came to the house one afternoon and asked me, "Mom, are there any kids out on the deck playing basketball today?"

I looked out the window and answered, "I don't see any."

"Oh, okay. I guess I will go out to play then."

I realized then that living in Alaska might be harder on my kids than I thought. I talked to Rick that night about the incident, and we decided it might be time for us to return to the lower forty-eight. With everything that happened to us, such as the hepatitis and the death of a student, we decided to return to our home in Lynden, Washington.

How did I leave my teaching years in Alaska? By having a circus! It was spring and the ice was breaking up on the river. People were in a good mood because they would soon be able to hunt for seal and catch fish for their winter food supply.

I decided to have a spring program for the village, and we prepared for our circus. I took some material I found in the storage room and made tutus for the girls who were going to be ballerinas. I asked the maintenance man for a long tube he might have in his shop to use for an elephant's nose. I also got a mophead to use for a lion's mane and I started sewing costumes. I found more muslin and old material from the musty storeroom and made the bodies for the elephant and lion. I procured a large two-by-four plank to use for someone to walk from side to side like he was on a tightrope. I knew there should be clowns, so I enlisted some of the older boys to wear overalls, and they were going to be fireman to put out a pretend blaze. I found some tempera paint and added soap to it so I could paint faces on the clowns, with a red nose, of course. We found a tall cardboard box and we painted a building. We cut out windows and put some yellow paper flames coming out of the windows. The boys borrowed a hose from the maintenance man and pretended to put out the fire. I had to have music, so I found a suitable tape, we practiced, and the circus was on. All the people in the village crowded into my classroom, and many of them sat on the floor since we didn't have enough chairs.

The elephant ran around the pretend ring, a lion tamer had a string whip and was training his lion to sit up. Then the girls came to do their ballet on the two-by-four and the tight rope walker pretended he was going to fall off the board. The finale included the clowns rushing in to put out the fire and throwing a bucket of confetti on it to put it out. There was much laughter and frivolity that day, and I am sure the villagers will never forget it. I know I will not, nor will my own two children who participated. What a way to leave a village and our glorious days in Alaska!

PART SIX

Adulting in the Lower Forty-Eight

CHAPTER 23

Our Days on the Reservation

Since we had just finished our career with the Bureau of Indian Affairs, we felt that teaching Native Americans in the lower forty-eight would be an easy transition to the real world. We were familiar with living with people from another culture, so we thought this was the right thing to do. We applied to teach at an Indian school in Omak, Washington, that was funded by the Bureau of Indian Affairs. It was not far from where both our parents lived in Spokane. We thought it would be nice to have both sets of grandparents near our little ones for a change. We interviewed with the Native American principal, got the jobs, and moved to Okanogan, Washington. The school was a boarding school for Native American children, and the caretakers were young people who were Jesuit volunteers. They stayed with the students during the week and most of the children went home on the weekends. Some students lived in their own homes in Omak and Okanogan who attended the school. I was assigned to teach sixth-grade reading classes and Rick taught a self-contained seventh-grade class. We were both in for an eye-opening experience.

We quickly found out that these students were not like Alaska Natives and were not quite as compliant as the students we were used to teaching. We noticed right away that when we had recess and two children were arguing on the playground, the students would form a large ring with joined hands so the students could battle it out physically within the ring. This started from the second grade on up and it was an everyday thing. We got used to it and taught the students the best way we knew how. They were just children after all, and most of them were delightful human beings we needed to nurture.

One of my sixth-grade students was very tall and it looked like he might even be growing a mustache. He seemed to pick on the younger children on the playground. I got tired of this, and one day as we were coming back into the classroom, I stopped him at the door and confronted him, "Donald, I want you to stop bothering the younger children at recess. This has to stop."

The other students heard me talk to him, and when Donald stepped inside the door, the students formed a ring around Donald and me as if we were going to duke it out. I couldn't believe they had done this, but I did not have time to think. My knees started shaking and I just stared at Donald until he lowered his head and sat down at his desk. I got called into the principal's office later that day, where Donald's parents sat facing me. I told his parents and the principal what he had been doing for several weeks and that I had asked him to stop doing that. Evidently, Donald was embarrassed and was not used to being called out for such behavior. The parents listened, and told me they would talk to Donald, and we all left the principal's office. It was a close call.

Another day, a student named Johnny came to my reading class. He was only in the fourth grade, but he was gifted in reading, so the fourth-grade teacher and the principal placed him in my sixth-grade reading class. He walked up to me and said, "Mrs. Gilmore, I can't work today. No one cares about me. My parents haven't been to pick me up for four weeks now."

I could see he was quite upset, and I told him that I cared about him, but of course that was not enough. I told him he could go sit under the table and rest while the sixth-grade class had reading. He did that, and in the middle of my class, I checked on Johnny, and he was curled up in the fetal position sound asleep. I had studied Abraham Maslow's *Hierarchy of Needs* (Maslow, 1954) paradigm in college and realized that although Johnny was gifted, he could not work that day because his basic needs were not being met. He was stuck on the ladder where a person needs the love from a family in order to move on to learning. I always remembered that incident as a physical example of what I learned in college. Johnny was eventually picked up by his parents for a home visit and his attitude toward school and reading improved over the year.

At the end of the year, as most teachers like to do, I planned a field trip for my sixth-grade reading class. I asked the principal to approve my plan to take the students to the Opera House in Spokane to see a ballet. After the ballet, we were going to go on some rides that were near the Opera House, left over from the World's Fair that had been held in Spokane. The students and I were excited to go, and I received permission slips from their parents for the big day. We boarded the bus and were on our way.

Now, the Opera House is a very nice venue, and as I took my students to the lobby of the building, two of my feisty boys decided to get in a fist fight right before the ballet. The other students did not have time to form a ring, and luckily I managed to break up the fight before we climbed the stairs to our seats. The students had never been to a ballet before, let alone the Opera House, and as we were sitting in our seats, some of the boys and girls put their feet up on the chairs that were in front of them. They proceeded to comb their hair and talk to their neighbors. I had them put their feet down, put away their combs, and watch the ballet. I thought to myself, *maybe it wasn't such a good idea to take my class to a ballet.* We managed to get through it and I took the students to the rides, where they were much happier. We sat and ate our sack lunches by the Spokane River and headed home on the bus.

Rick had a fairly good year teaching his seventh-grade students, although he said they were definitely a little harder to teach than the Alaska Natives. Although the difficult times stand out in our minds, children are children and there were many great moments as well. Parents always want the best for their children, and when we taught there, the school was just realizing that they needed to mix academics with the local Native American culture. This gave the students an appreciation and awareness of their own culture as well as the academics that are required to advance in the modern day world.

At the end of the school year, we decided to move back to our home in Lynden, as we had been renting it out to others who had not paid the rent. We were back in our dream home.

CHAPTER 24

We'll Stay Forever

I knew I would not be content to stay in our beloved split-level home on our lovely tree-lined street, as I had tried that already and it did not work out for me. So, I got a job teaching at Assumption Elementary School in Bellingham, Washington. I taught kindergarten there for two years, and since I had taught band in Alaska, I became the music and band teacher for grades kindergarten through the eighth grade. For me, I found that I wasn't the kindergarten type. The children were darling, but I needed a little more stimulation than teaching beginning sounds and numbers. I also found teaching kindergarten was hard on my back since I was bending down all the time beside their little desks to help them with their work. God bless kindergarten teachers. It is not an easy job.

What saved me was that I interned as an elementary principal for one year, and the formal principal was a lovely nun from Seattle, Washington. She was kind and helped show me the ropes for becoming a principal. The other part that I really liked was being the music and band teacher for all grades. My biggest achievement in my second year was putting on an all-school musical for the Christmas program. It was not without a slight glitch. As we were having our last rehearsal before the real night, we had all the students gathered in the gym. There were probably two hundred students, and since it was held in the gym, someone had left a few basketballs in the bleachers. As I worked with the younger students, the eighth-grade boys, who were sitting in the top bleachers, started bouncing the basketballs. I stopped conducting the fourth-grade choir and turned around with a scowl and said very loudly, "Will you boys who have balls please bring them down here this instant."

You don't say that to the whole student body without having a few snickers, especially from the eighth-grade boys. Luckily, on the night of the program, everyone performed the way they were supposed to and the musical was well received by the audience.

My husband had several jobs to help out the family while he was attending school at Western Washington University. He wanted to receive a master's degree in student personnel, which basically meant that he would be a financial aid officer for the university. He enjoyed some of his graduate classes, but at the same time, he got a part-time job as a US Customs Inspector in Blaine, Washington, which was a major port of entry from Canada. While he was working at the border, he checked to see what his salary would be as a financial aid officer with a master's degree, and the person in charge said that it would pay $16,000 a year. At the same time, the people at the border liked his work ethic and suggested that he become a full-time inspector. He inquired about his salary as a customs inspector and they told him it would be $32,000 per year with possible overtime shifts. Now, we had a family of six, and it was surprising that a master's degree salary was half the salary of a customs inspector. Guess what? Rick put in for a full-time position and got the job. Where was it? In Eastern Montana, near the small town of Plentywood, Montana. We had to leave our home once again to sights unknown, but it was for the good of the family. We left that winter to arrive at the Port of Raymond, where they had a nice brick house waiting for us. The amazing thing was that we arrived at our new home on Christmas Eve. I had ordered Christmas presents ahead of time from a Sears catalog where you ordered goods from a magazine and later received them in the mail. I didn't know if the presents would get there in time, but I hoped for the best.

When we walked into our new quarters, we were very surprised to see a lighted and decorated Christmas tree. There were two other families who lived in adjoining houses at the border, and knowing that we were arriving on Christmas Eve, they had prepared our house and Christmas tree for us. For this, we will be forever grateful.

I called Van and Marie Tvedt, who owned the Sears outlet store in Plentywood, and asked them if our presents were at their store. They said, "Yes, and we'll go there and unlock it for you so you can get the presents for your children."

I couldn't believe that people would be so kind to leave their Christmas Eve celebration, drive to the store, and help us pick up our presents. What a wonderful introduction to our life in Plentywood, Montana.

The children enrolled in school and were treated like celebrities. I don't think too many big families like ours moved to Plentywood very often. They seemed very content in their new environment, and Rick got very busy working at the border. I couldn't stay home again, so I got a job working in a grocery store in Plentywood. I was a checker and eventually ended up painting a large sign on the outside of the building called John's Warehouse. The owners of the store, John and Darlene Vogt, were upstanding citizens, and when someone couldn't pay for their groceries, they let them charge it and pay later. I got to see the great humanity of the people I worked for. Eventually, I acquired a job teaching fifth- and sixth-grade science at Plentywood Elementary, where I remained for five years.

CHAPTER 25

No, I Don't

I loved my job teaching science because I had to learn more than I taught about all things related to science, such as: layers of the earth, different types of rocks, constellations, how to do science experiments, and many other new concepts.

One incident stands out in my mind from the time I taught at Plentywood Elementary. I had just come home from school, exhausted as usual, and I heard a knock at the door. I opened it and there stood my friend Judy Larson with sad puppy-dog eyes.

"Hi, Deanna. I don't want to bother you, but I have a serious situation on my hands. Hans and I were down by the creek today, and we saw a mother raccoon who was drowned lying on the shore. We looked a little closer, and there were three baby raccoons who were trying to nurse from her. We know they will die if we don't bring them home and feed them. Since you are a science teacher, we think you might be an excellent person to take one of the babies to help it stay alive. What do you think?"

Who wouldn't want to help a baby raccoon stay alive? I remembered that several people kept raccoons for pets in the Palouse Country in Washington where I grew up.

"Sure, I will take one. Maybe when it gets a little older, I can take it to my science class and share it with my students."

She went to her car, and I watched through the window as she brought the scrawny little black and white animal to the house. As Judy handed it to me, I could see that it was about the shape of a medium-sized rat. It didn't have a lot of fur, but I could see the black and white stripes of its body.

I quickly got a Turkish towel and wrapped the baby raccoon in my arms to keep it warm. It peered up at me with black beady eyes. I could hardly wait to show my children our new family pet.

"Pat, Amy, Tara, Brian, come see! I have a new pet."

The kids were downstairs playing on Pat's waterbed and they rushed up the minute they heard the word "pet." They stared down at the bundle in my arms.

"What is it?" Pat asked.

"It is a baby raccoon and its mother drowned. We must feed it to keep it alive. We will get an eye dropper and give it some warm milk. It will grow up with us and be a cute pet. Some friends of mine in Washington had a pet raccoon and they loved it. They can get into mischief, though. Who wants to take him?"

"I will," said Pat.

I handed over the blue bundle of towel and raccoon to my oldest son, who was in the eighth grade. He took it downstairs to his bed and Amy, Tara, and Brian followed him. They each had a turn holding it for a little while, then Pat took over again.

We didn't know if it was a boy or girl, and we weren't going to try to find out. The kids and I guessed it was a him, so we named him Ricky Raccoon. Their dad's name was Rick, so it couldn't have been more appropriate.

The real Rick Gilmore arrived home a little later and I wasn't sure how I was going to break the news to him that we had a new pet and his name was Ricky.

Rick went downstairs to see the new addition to the family. Being a pet lover, it wasn't hard to convince him that we had to save the baby's life. As he held up his namesake, he said, "I guess you are here to stay, little fellow."

We left Ricky in a cardboard box during the day while we were at work and school. He grew bigger because he was nourished by the warm milk and love we fed him. When our children came home from school, they rushed down to see who could grab him first. Patrick even slept with him at night and I would find Ricky curled up under Pat's neck in the morning.

As he got bigger, I thought it was time to take Ricky to school to share him with students in my fifth- and sixth-grade science class. So, one day, I wrapped Ricky in a clean towel, put him in a tall cardboard box and took him in the car to our elementary school. While heading there, I was thinking about how the students would react to having a live baby raccoon in their classes.

The bell rang and in came the fifth graders. They didn't sit at their desks but moved quickly to the front of the room, where I had placed the box holding the prize. They scrambled to pet him and I told them to take turns. They enjoyed touching Ricky and feeling his wiry hair. Class ended and it was the same scene for the sixth graders. They enjoyed seeing Ricky up close, and not just seeing a raccoon on TV. The day ended, I took Ricky home, and he slept with Pat again that night. I rested happily knowing that I had shared a great learning experience with my science students.

The next day, I left Ricky home and school returned to normal. I had to get back to the real stuff and teach about the different layers of the earth in my science class. I was busy teaching about the crust, mantle, and inner and outer cores of the earth when I heard a knock on the door. I opened it and there stood the superintendent of the school, Mr. Richards, along with a game warden from the Fish and Wildlife Department. I recognized his olive green uniform.

Mr. Richard's asked me, "Do you have a raccoon at school?"

I answered in all honesty, "No, I don't."

I failed to tell him that I did have one at school the day before. Since I didn't have a raccoon in my classroom, they turned and left my door.

One of the students asked, "What did they want Mrs. Gilmore?"

"Oh, nothing. Let's get back to work," I replied.

As I continued teaching about the mantle, I could hardly concentrate. Did I do the right thing? They said, "Do you have a raccoon at school?" And of course, I didn't.

When I went home after school that night, I waited until the kids were asleep and I tiptoed downstairs to check on Ricky the Raccoon. There he was, with his little arm wrapped around my son's neck.

The next day, as I was teaching fifth-grade science, a booming voice came over the loudspeaker.

"Will anyone who has seen or touched a raccoon in the last two days please come down to the office!"

My eyes got big, and I knew the jig was up. I asked the twenty-six students in my fifth grade science class to stand up and follow me in a line. We were going to the principal's office.

With my head facing the ground and a frown crossing my forehead, the students huddled behind me when we arrived at the principal's office.

Mr. Carson was sitting back in his office chair with his arms folded looking very stern, "I thought you said you didn't have a raccoon at school, Mrs. Gilmore."

"I didn't, the day you asked me," I answered with remorse.

He told me to take the children back to my classroom and said he wanted to see me after school.

I felt like a kid who had been caught with her hand in the cookie jar and just a little bit nauseous.

I finished the day teaching sixth graders more about the inner and outer cores of the earth, but my mind wasn't really on it.

I visited with Mr. Carson after school and he told me that raccoons in that area of Montana were known to carry rabies. He also said that Fish and Wildlife personnel would be coming to my house after school to pick up Ricky the Raccoon.

Mr. Carson gave me this grave news. "They are going to kill your baby raccoon and send its head to Helena, Montana, where they will check to see if it has rabies. If it does, you, your family, and your students will have to get a series of rabies shots in the stomach."

I was just sick. Who wouldn't be? How was I going to tell my children what was going to happen to Ricky? That evening after school, I told Pat, Amy, Tara and Brian, that I was so sorry, but some men from Fish and Wildlife were going to take Ricky away from us and give him a more natural environment to live in. The children were stunned and all went downstairs to commiserate on Pat's waterbed.

About 4:00 p.m., the doorbell rang and I went downstairs and took Ricky from Pat's arms and brought him up to the men in uniform. Pat had watery eyes as I carried Ricky away and handed him to the men in the drab green uniforms.

We were all sad that night at our house, and especially me, because I was worried that if the raccoon had rabies, each one of my students would have to have the rabies shots. Not only were they going to be painful, but each shot cost $360. For the fifty students who touched him, that would have been $18,000 out of the district's pocket . . . or mine. I didn't know how it would go, but I thought I might lose my teaching job over this and I loved my job.

As it happened, my parents were visiting us from Spokane during all these events. They had come over to spend time with their grandchildren. I was very worried and I didn't feel like cooking or eating anything. As a family, we decided to go out for pizza, and before we left, we heard an announcer on the television saying, "In Plentywood, Montana, a student brought a raccoon to school," (*at least they didn't say a teacher,* I thought).

I was so embarrassed I didn't even hear the rest of the announcement. I imagine the reporter was reminding people that raccoons can carry rabies. I walked slowly down the stairs, followed by my family, who were surprised that they heard our school mentioned on television.

My father, who was with us, had a great sense of humor and often knew how to lighten the load during a terrible situation. As we were on the sidewalk heading to the car, he took his sweater and placed it over his head as if he were with a criminal and didn't want to be seen with such a person. I couldn't help but laugh as I stepped into the car.

When we arrived at the pizza parlor, I still couldn't eat and all I could think about was having my students getting their painful shots in the stomach and getting fired. I had asked the Fish and Wildlife personnel to let me know what they found out about Ricky having rabies as soon as they heard. They said they would call me the next day. Of course, I didn't sleep much that night.

As I walked into the school cafeteria the next day, I did the 'walk of shame' and I felt like everyone was staring at me as if I really were a criminal. I felt like saying out loud, "I didn't know. People in Washington raised raccoons as pets when I grew up there, and if I thought it would be harmful, do you think I would let the baby raccoon sleep with my son?"

But, of course, I didn't say anything. I was just hoping that the students and staff were thinking about something else rather than me and Ricky the raccoon.

As I walked through the door after a very long day of teaching, the phone rang. Ring! Ring! It was the fateful call from Fish and Wildlife. Over the phone, a wildlife office announced that Ricky the Raccoon, though dead now, did not have rabies. I was in the clear along with my fifty fifth- and sixth-grade students. I took some long breaths and almost cried. They weren't going to get those horrible shots and I might keep my teaching job. Which I did keep!

The Christmas after the incident, my father sent me a present in the mail. It was a stuffed momma raccoon holding a baby raccoon in her arms. Another laugh to lighten my load.

MOMMA RACCOON AND HER BABY, BY CHLOE GILMORE

CHAPTER 26

Teacher Loses Her Cool

The students in Plentywood were very nice and easy to teach. Located in Eastern Montana, Plentywood was a farming community with supporting businesses, restaurants, and stores to help sustain the population of 2,000 people. The parents of the students were very interested in having their children succeed in school and they supported the teachers in their pursuit to do so. Of course, as any teacher knows, you are going to have one or two kids in your class who will give you trouble. No matter how young or old, that is just a 'rule of thumb,' as people say. In my five years of teaching fifth- and sixth-grade science to the students there, I had very few hostile encounters with the parents there. They knew I worked hard and wanted the best for their children.

As teachers, we are expected to toe the line and be examples of calmness and professionalism in the classroom. The hardest part about teaching is maintaining discipline and structure in the classroom. Over the years I attended many workshops on classroom management which were designed to help teachers.

Prior to my fifth year of teaching fifth and sixth graders science at Plentywood Elementary, I enrolled in a classroom management course at a branch campus of Montana State University. At the time, this course followed the teachings of some expert in classroom management, and I left summer school knowing that if I followed the suggestions in this textbook, I would have no discipline problems in the classroom. In those days, we might use the term, 'Gung ho!' I was ready.

Before school started, I made posters for both of my classes with everyone's name on the poster. I remember that I had a system of checks for negative behaviors. One of the consequences of receiving three checks was that the student had to call home and tell the parent or guardian what they had done wrong, then stay after school for fifteen minutes that day. This meant that they had to miss the bus and the parent was obligated to come pick them up after school.

Well, things were working very well for the most part. I did have trouble keeping up with the positive and negative behavior checks, but I had very few people stay after school . . . until one day! I was teaching an important concept about science in my fifth-grade class, and one of my female students wasn't paying attention, and she kept touching the neck of the boy sitting in front of her. I asked her to stop and pay attention to what I was saying, but she continued with the behavior. I walked over to the poster and silently put a check after her name. At a glance, I noticed that she had three checks and would have to call her parents.

Without raising her hand, she blurted out, "My dad said that if I got another check, he was going to come and see you."

This made my blood boil, and suddenly I shoved the podium I was standing behind and it flew down the middle of the newly waxed floor. In no uncertain terms, I replied, "Well, bring him on!" The students on either side of the room sat there stunned, and I said very loudly, "Sometimes you kids act like assholes!"

In my nineteen years of teaching, I had never said a swear word to my whole class because that wasn't the right thing to do. You don't punish the whole class for something one person said. I was shocked at myself that I had let that word slip through my lips.

Things returned to a quiet standstill for the rest of the period, then the students left for their next class. I knew I would have some repercussions for my actions, so at the end of the day, I turned off the lights and sat at one of the desks in sorrow. I had committed a teacher sin!

A few minutes after school was out, I saw the parents of the maligned girl walk past my open classroom door headed toward the elementary principal. About twenty minutes later, he called me down to the office for a little chat. I told him that I was sorry, and that in my nineteen years of teaching I had never said a swear word to my whole class. I told him I would never do it again, and after hearing my side of the story, he told me I had to apologize to my class the next day. I thought the principal may have felt some of the same things I spewed that day because he let me off gently. I will never know.

CHAPTER 27

Parlez-Vous Francais

My husband is an adventurer and I am a little bit the same. After five years in Plentywood, he came home one day and asked me if I would like to move to Montreal, Quebec, where he would be an inspector at the Dorval Airport? What?! Move again, after we have already been established and engrained in the culture of Plentywood, Montana?

My two older children, Patrick and Amy, had already flown the nest and were busy attending college, Patrick at Montana State University and Amy at cosmetology school in Billings, Montana. Tara was going to be a freshman in high school and Brian was in the sixth grade. We were just renting our home at the time, so it was possible.

Montreal sounded exotic to me and somewhat exciting. I said I would go, thinking our two younger ones would be okay with it. It would be an adventure for them and also a cultural experience, which never hurt anyone.

So off we went. Pat helped us drive out there and it was a three day trip. Rick drove the U-Haul and I helped with the kids. Brian rode with his big brother Pat and our old English sheepdog, Oliver, sat in the back seat. Along the way, it seemed that Oliver wasn't able to go to the bathroom very well on the trip, and we, not knowing what was wrong, just hoped that once we arrived at our home, he would be alright. Not so. Reminiscent of the movie *Vacation* starring Chevy Chase, Oliver died in the back seat of the car.

When we arrived at our new home in Beaconsfield, Quebec, Rick dug a grave and buried Oliver in the back yard of our rental home . . . hopefully deep enough that no one ever discovered the bones of our beloved American dog.

Now, going to school in Montreal was another story. We enrolled Tara in an English-speaking school called McDonalds, where both English-speaking and French-speaking students attended. Since Quebec province required schools to teach in both French and English, that is what they did.

It was Tara's first day of French class, and when she came home she said the teacher told her the assignment was to write her autobiography in French. Tara politely replied, "I don't know how to speak French."

The teacher replied, "Do it anyway."

Nice way to start the French class. Of course, the next day Tara turned in a blank sheet of paper and received an F for the grade. Another day, the teacher passed out a quiz all written in French and Tara again said, "I don't know how to read the questions in French."

She received another F. There were no accommodations or special help for students who spoke English as their first language. French as a second language classes were non-existent and Tara felt terrible receiving her F grades.

Brian got along a little bit better at his Catholic school in Beacons-field, as he didn't have to take tests or write his autobiography in French in the sixth grade. He was a good basketball player in Plentywood before he left to come to Montreal, so he helped to show the other students how to play the game. Hockey was their national sport, so he became a star of their basketball team.

During the winter, Brian went to the public tennis courts in Beaconsfield where we lived and there he learned how to skate and play hockey. In the winter months, the locals flooded the tennis courts and turned them into hockey rinks. Brian also learned some French from the adults who played there.

I became bored staying home, so I took the subway to McGill University where I signed up for classes. I thought about becoming a school counselor so I signed up for four courses at McGill. The registrar called me into her office as I was enrolling for classes and said, "I think you should not take four classes this semester. Are you sure you want to do this?"

I answered, "Well, I was always an A student in my courses in the States so I think I can do it."

"If that is what you want to do, alright then."

I should have listened to her. McGill was the hardest university I ever attended. I took a course in abnormal psychology where we studied the DSM-4 (Manual of Standards for Diagnosing mental illness, 1994) and had to answer questions about mental health. In addition, my other courses were psychology, social psychology, and statistics. Halfway into my classes, I discovered that McGill had a medical school, and courses such as statistics were meant to weed out people who wanted to become doctors, or MDs. Statistics was especially hard for me and I had to get a tutor to help me through. I received a B for the grade and I was happy to get that. I received As in the other courses.

After receiving my grades and realizing that I had passed, I decided to take the next semester off and rest my case for becoming a school counselor. I already had a master's degree in education administration, so I decided to concentrate on that area.

I breathed a sigh of relief during the winter months because I didn't have to go to school, but I had a few incidents with the French-speaking people that made me feel like returning to the United States. This was during the political period when the French-speaking people wanted to secede from Canada and make their own country. Therefore, the Francophiles weren't always kind to the Anglophiles who lived there, especially if they couldn't speak French. While I struggled, Rick was doing fine at the airport and in the spring, he received an award from US Customs for being the inspector of the year. He knew I was unhappy, so he put in for a job at the border where he had worked in Plentywood and got the job. For a change, he followed me this time, back to Plentywood where I felt like we belonged.

CHAPTER 28

Back to Big Sky Country

When we moved back to Plentywood, of course my former teaching job was filled. In the meantime I took a job at a sheltered workshop for developmentally disabled adults and had an eye-opening experience while working there. Our clients ranged in ages from twenty-five to sixty, and they had varying degrees of disabilities. They are all God's children, so I worked with them with compassion and tried to help them move along in life.

At times, it was very difficult and when an older adult became unruly, we would have to use the Mandt hold to restrain them. The Mandt hold was developed by David Mandt in 1975 as a way to safely restrain someone who may harm other clients and the staff to keep them from being injured. I had training for that but I wasn't used to being physical with my elementary students so this was hard for me to do both physically and mentally. I left the workshop with migraine headaches at times because of the stress of the job.

I also knew the great rewards that came when one of our clients got a job at the local grocery store or when a young couple were permitted to be married because they were high functioning and could live on their own. I cared a lot about them . . . maybe too much. It takes a special person to care for and teach special people.

This job took a toll on my health, so I decided to apply for a teaching job forty-five minutes from Plentywood in Scobey, Montana. I knew it would be a long drive, but I wanted to teach again. I applied, interviewed, and was given the job of teaching Title I for students who struggled with reading in the middle and high school classes. I enjoyed this assignment very much as I was able to practice some of the things I learned in college regarding teaching reading. The main thing I remembered from my courses was that it helps struggling readers to read their materials aloud in class. Since most of the students I had in class were in the same predicament, they didn't mind reading slowly in front of others. I was home again. I loved my students.

One of the things I didn't realize about teaching middle school students was how volatile and unsettled they can be. I had only taught elementary grades up until then, so this was new to me. One day, one of my teenage students came stomping in the room, threw her books on the floor, and proceeded to lay her head down on top of her desk. She cried very loudly so we couldn't read our chapter book aloud. I knelt down beside her and asked her what was wrong. She sobbed, "My boyfriend just broke up with me," with more tears, and when she finally sat up, a puddle of water covered the entire top of her desk and it was flowing over the sides like a waterfall.

I asked one of the other students in her group to grab some paper towels. We wiped off her desk, and when she finally calmed down, we went on with class. I had a lot to learn about the upper grades.

In the second semester I taught Title I, I had an older student who wanted to attend college but he struggled with reading and writing. He knew he wouldn't be able to go if he didn't pass the American College Testing (ACT). I spent a few extra hours with him helping with certain math and reading concepts. A few weeks later he took the test. I had forgotten about him and as I was busy teaching my reading group, but one day I saw the shadow of a tall figure standing next to me. He didn't bother to excuse himself and blurted out. "Mrs. Gilmore, I passed. I can go to college now."

I stood up and with a big grin, I joined him in the celebration. These are the kinds of moments that make teaching worthwhile.

At the end of my second year of teaching Title 1, I was honored with the "Teacher of the Year" award from the National Honor Society of Scobey High School. It was also during that same summer I heard that the elementary principal was retiring. I hadn't told too many people that I had obtained my master's in education administration, so I quietly applied for the job. After interviews with several teachers and the school board, I was offered the position as a principal/teacher. There had been a reduction in enrollment over the years I was there, so the school board thought I might be able to combine the principal's job with teaching.

I accepted and moved my Donald Duck and Mickey Mouse collection of figures into the main office, where I worked as the high school principal with Superintendents Mr. David Hart and Mr. Gerald Roger. They were both wonderful administrators and we all got along quite well. Half the battle of teaching is to put aside any jealousies and comparisons and realize that you are all there for the students. I was in charge of the Gifted and Talented Program and the Odyssey of the Mind, which challenged students to think outside the box and expand their resources.

Being the fifth-grade science teacher and acting as a principal was a little bit of a challenge. There was a lot to do, and sometimes one of my jobs might have been a little short-changed. We can only do so much.

I recall this one incident when I was trying to do both jobs, both teaching and being an administrator. To give my students and me a break after noon recess, I had the students lay their heads down on the desk while I read a chapter book aloud to them, using voices and the proper inflection. This particular time, I was reading *Freckle Juice* by Judy Blume (1971). In the story, Andrew Marcus wants to have freckles like his friend, Nicky Lane. Sharon, one of their classmates, tells Andrew that she knows a recipe for freckle juice and that she will give him the recipe if he gives her fifty cents for it. Andrew is only in the second grade and so he falls for it and gives her the money for the made-up recipe, which consists of the following: grape juice, vinegar, mustard, mayonnaise, lemon juice, pepper, salt, ketchup, olive oil, and onion.

Just as I was reading this part aloud, I had the bright idea to make the freckle juice and have my students try it in class. I always believed in taking advantage of bringing stories to life, so that night I went home and rounded up all the materials I would need for the freckle juice. I smelled the olive oil that was in my cupboard and I thought it smelled a little bit rancid, something like the seal oil I smelled in Alaska. But I thought olive oil lasted a long time, so I didn't buy a new bottle at the local grocery store. I knew we wouldn't want to taste too much of this concoction, so I bought small ketchup cups at the store to hold our freckle juice.

The next day, I was so excited to make the freckle juice with the students that I almost forgot to read that part of the story again. I wrote the ingredients on the board and I had different students come up and drop the ingredients into a large white bowl. One of the students stirred it with a large wooden spoon and then I scooped up the freckle juice into each container and put it on their desks. I also made some for myself, of course. I wasn't going to be left out of this fun.

We were going to drink it on the count of three, so one-two-three and down it went. It was disgusting and the students were gagging and running up to the wastebasket to spit out the contents of their stomachs. I almost threw up myself, but being the adult in the group,

I knew I should not.

We talked about the experience a little bit before I read on in the book. We did not want to dwell on it as we still had a bad taste in our mouths.

That night, as I was feeding my own children, I received a phone call from a parent. She said her little girl would not be coming to class the next day because she had an emergency appendectomy that evening in the local hospital.

I was in a little bit of shock because I knew from my own experience with my son that certain things you eat can prompt an appendicitis attack. I thought immediately of the freckle juice we had swallowed that same day, and the rather pungent smell of the olive oil that was contained therein. Was I the cause of this attack and subsequent surgery? I did not mention it to the parent on the phone and I hoped her daughter would not talk about it either. To ease my conscience, I bought flowers and took them to the little girl that evening after she recovered from her surgery. The parents were nice and the little girl was too weak to mention such things as consuming freckle juice earlier in the day. I never heard any more about it from the little girl or her parents, and to this day, I will never know if the freckle juice and the old olive oil brought on the appendix attack. So much for bright ideas and experiential learning!

CHAPTER 29
Erin Go Braugh (Ireland Forever)

During my fourth year as principal/teacher for the Scobey School District, Rick came home from his job as the Port Director in Whitetail, Montana, and told me had accepted a job to be an immigration inspector in Shannon, Ireland. He asked me if I wanted to go.

"Ireland? The US Government would pay for our move??!! Of course I will go with you." I said.

He had not told me about applying for the job beforehand because he thought he might not get it. But get it, he did, and we were off to Ireland. Erin go Braugh!

It was a perfect time for us to have a new experience in the land of castles, beautiful scenery, and Irish music. Tara was married to a wonderful young man who was the son of the elementary principal in Plentywood, Montana, and Brian was attending college at Montana State University in Bozeman, Montana. We had no children to take care of and only green pastures ahead.

We flew to Ireland and landed in Shannon; the very place Rick would be working. I did not have a job so I had the luxury of taking in the culture on my own.

We stayed in a beautiful hotel near the Bunratty castle for a few days until I found a house we could rent. At the time, Brian was on a break between semesters at Montana State University, so he flew over and joined us at the hotel. It was hard finding a home to rent and most of them were farm homes and a little on the rough side. I was discouraged, but one day the realtor told me about a home someone wanted to rent that had the furniture already in it. I told him I would like to see it. It was in Cratloe, County Clare. The next day he drove me there and I could not believe it. It was a mansion, like I had never seen before, with built-in mahogany dressers, exquisite tile floors, and a bar to entertain guests. It was all furnished and we found out that the owner was a bride whose husband had been killed in a lorry (truck) accident and she couldn't bear to live in her home anymore. She left all of the furnishings and moved to an apartment in Limerick, and we were the beneficiaries.

We lived very close to the Catholic church in Cratloe called the Church of St. John. It was built in 1791 and was only one of three 'barn' churches in Ireland built during penal times. It was a period when Catholics were not allowed to practice their religion, so they disguised the church as a barn so they could hold Mass there.

I met some very nice women at the church who proceeded to show me around Ireland and take me to all the castles in the area. Their names were Kayleigh Carmondy, Mary McDermott, and Teresa McNamara, all 'full on' Irish names. Since we lived there for two and a half years, I became very close to these women, as they helped take up my days in Ireland.

Something I found amusing about Kayleigh and Teresa was that we would be out listening to Irish music and having a Guinness beer and all of a sudden they would say, "I've had enough of this diddle dee dee music. Let's get out of here."

Here I was, a visiting American who was thoroughly enjoying the Irish music, and they had heard it so often over their lives that it was not novel to them. They preferred listening to modern music.

We lived there for two and a half years, and toward the end of my second year, I got kind of tired of looking at castles and going out for tea, so I applied for a job teaching in County Cork.

I don't remember how I learned about the job, but I drove down to Charleville, County Cork, and visited with the lady Principal of Holy Family School there. This was a school for special education students from grades kindergarten to grade eight. We visited for a while and she decided to hire me to teach ten eighth-grade students, eight boys and two girls, in a self-contained classroom. She told me that teachers in Ireland had to speak Gaelic to get a teaching license, but special education teachers were not required to learn Gaelic. That was the only reason she was able to hire me as an American.

I was happy to be teaching again, but a little concerned as I had never taught special education in America. I had worked at a workshop for developmentally disabled adults, so that allowed me to take this job.

Luckily, I had a teacher's aide with me in the classroom who already knew the students. They had various developmental and physical disabilities, but I found them delightful to teach. One of the boys couldn't say Deanna, so he would always come up to me and say, "Anna, Anna, please play the piano for us."

My contribution to the school was my ability to play the piano and lead the students in singing songs they already knew from Disney movies. Many students in Ireland had seen *Mary Poppins*, so I had the students sing various songs from the movie many times over.

The special education teachers at Holy Family School were extremely caring and never complained about their jobs. I was impressed by their dedication to the students, and as teachers they represented the country of Ireland in a very positive manner.

When it came time for us to return to the United States, my Irish friends from Cratloe held a party for us at the community hall. They had a banner posted that said *"American Wake."* I asked my friend Kayleigh what this meant, and she told me that when the Irish people emigrated to America their friends held a wake before they left. They thought it would be the last time we would see them.

The ladies I taught with drove up from Charleville to attend the party, and several women I met in Ireland and their husbands also attended our wake. They all went together and purchased some beautiful Waterford Crystal wine glasses for us. We found the Irish people to be very kind and lots of fun to be around. We were very thankful for our years living in Ireland.

OUR MANOR HOUSE IN IRELAND

CHAPTER 30

Wilderness Sub

After two and a half years, we returned to the United States, where Rick was hired as an immigration inspector at the port of entry in Northport, Washington. I was a tagalong with no children to care for because they were all grown and on their way.

I got restless being a stay-at-home grandma, so I applied to be a substitute teacher for the Northport School. Northport is in a beautiful area with tall fir and cedar trees on either side of the highway as you drive into the center of the town. On the lower end of Northport is a huge lake called Roosevelt Lake, which is a tributary of the Columbia River. We lived in a log cabin outside of town in the woods, where we often heard coyotes howling in the night.

It was not long before I received a call from the school superintendent to come in for an interview. She wanted me to take a long-term sub position since the seventh grade teacher was going to have a baby, and she needed me to teach for three months. The superintendent was a very pleasant, capable educator with young children herself, and I knew I would get along with her. I took the job.

Boy, was I in for an eye-opening experience! At the time, there were only around 270 people living in the area and marijuana was not legal to have or smoke at the time. Since there were so many places to hide out in the woods, some of the residents partook of the substance on a regular basis. In my younger days, I would have called some of the residents "hippies," but at that time, we said they were living an "alternative lifestyle." I even attended a Barter Faire outside of Northport, where certain brownies and drug paraphernalia were sold out in the open.

As the permanent seventh-grade teacher took her leave, I began teaching the seventh-grade class. I would say that some of the students were a little 'rough around the edges.'

In the middle of teaching an English lesson, one of the girl students stood up and walked out of the classroom.

I asked her, "What are you doing?"

She answered nonchalantly, "I was just talking to my cousin to see if I was going to have a sleepover this weekend."

With a scowl on my face, I said, "Well, you just can't get up and walk outside the classroom when I am teaching."

She just shrugged her shoulders and sat down.

I had a hard time keeping the seventh graders' attention, so I decided to try something different. We were studying a shortened version of *Romeo and Juliet*, so I told the students we were going to have a special project. I checked out the video cameras from the office and said that we were going to tape our own version of *Romeo and Juliet*. I told them that the boys were going to be the Montagues to represent Romeo and the girls were going to be the Capulets to represent Juliet. I said they could film their parts on the weekend.

I let them meet in groups to plan their skits. I heard the boys discussing the fact that they were going to jump over the roofs of the local houses. That seemed okay to me, but one of the leaders came up to me and asked, "Mrs. Gilmore, is it all right if we use real guns for our play?"

"Of course not," I answered, and I knew right then and there that I had to call a halt to these shenanigans. "In fact, we are going to cancel this assignment. The video is off!"

I picked up the cameras and returned them quickly to the library.

I struggled to complete my last month of teaching seventh graders there, but I finished the task. By no means was I a quitter. The last day I taught, I drove home, plopped down on my couch, and said to Rick, "My days of subbing are over. What should I do now?"

CHAPTER 31

Unpacking Academia

"Well, you always wanted to get your doctorate. Why don't you look into that?" Those words came out of the mouth of my feminist husband who was encouraging me to do my own thing.

"But I might have to leave you to go to school!" I exclaimed.

"Well, the kids are all gone, so what is your excuse? You can drive back to see me on the weekends if you want to."

Here was my chance to achieve the dream of becoming a real college professor like I pretended to be when I taught classes as an undergraduate at Eastern Washington University.

I checked with Eastern but they did not offer a doctorate in education. I then read the guidelines for getting into the program at Washington State University and sure enough, one of the requirements was to be a resident on the campus to receive your doctorate. I took the plunge and drove five and a half hours from Northport to Pullman, Washington, to apply. While visiting with the registrar, he mentioned that I might be able to be a teaching assistant for other professors at the university to help pay my way through school. He checked something on his computer, made a call, and set up an interview with the children's literature professor for the same day. He knew I had driven a long way to apply.

I visited with Dr. Ingmar Keegan that very afternoon, and after talking to me for about an hour, she asked me if I was able to teach summer school in a few weeks because she wanted to go on vacation. Of course, I said, "Yes."

Dr. Keegan handed me the large textbook she used to teach children's literature to preservice teachers, along with a few other articles, and I was on my way. I was thrilled to have this opportunity not only to learn from new courses, but to be able to teach undergraduates and make some money at the same time. I could hardly contain myself as I drove home to give Rick the great news. It was a day of rejoicing!

I prepared for my children's literature classes and that was no problem. I followed Dr. Keegan's syllabus and felt comfortable in that role. What really hit me was returning to college after being out for so many years. I took four graduate-level classes and I hadn't been to college since the 1970s. A lot had changed and I realized I had a steep learning curve ahead of me. For instance, I hadn't written an academic paper since 1973, and I had to have a classmate show me how to use a mouse. The only mouse I knew before that time scurried around the house and made me jump on a chair. The other problem was that different professors used different platforms for their courses. I had to learn how to use a PC for one class and an Apple Mac for another class, and they are not the same. With help from my classmates, I learned both platforms in order to pass my courses.

Since I was working on a Ph.D. (Doctor of Philosophy) I had to declare a major, and I chose English as I was going to receive a Ph.D. in literacy education. In addition, I took many courses in research, the hardest being qualitative and quantitative research, which included hands-on projects, all while teaching two three-hour courses in children's literature.

It was during one of my English classes that a professor said, "Now, let's unpack that concept."

I did not know what he meant by that, as I had only known the term to mean unpack my luggage after I returned from a trip. The term was used by more than one professor and I thought to myself, *why don't they just say, "Now, let's figure out what this means."* The other two terms that were thrown around were "segue," as in "This is a great segue into my next subject" (meaning to change the subject), and "vis-à-vis," as in via this new thought.

I still hear the term 'unpack it' to this day on TV as journalists try to sound super educated when they speak. When I hear the term on the news, my husband always turns to me and says, "That's your favorite phrase, isn't it?"

At one point during my years of teaching courses and taking four courses a semester, I remember going to my office, lying down on the rug, and crying. I thought to myself *I can't do this. It is too much.* But I got up off the floor and plodded through the courses and started working on my dissertation. With the help of my chair, I decided to study how children learned literacy in two home schools compared to two public schools. The title of my dissertation was "Home School and Public School Contexts and How They Affect Reading Attitudes: A Qualitative Study." I spent over one hundred hours in the field at two home schools, where I studied the reading habits of two fourth-grade children. I also observed and wrote notes on the reading habits and teaching methods of fourth-grade students in two different public schools.

Suffice it to say that I wrote a two-hundred-fifty-page dissertation and defended it in front of a large committee with personal friends and family in attendance. After I was finished, I had to leave the room, as did my guests, and after some deliberation, I was asked to walk back into the presentation room, where they declared that I had passed and could now be addressed as Dr. Gilmore.

That summer, at the age of fifty-nine, I was hooded by the chair of my committee as my family members cheered from the balcony. After the graduation ceremony, I hosted a buffet lunch to thank my mentors and the faculty who taught and supported me throughout the process.

A few weeks after the ceremony, I was called into the dean's office and he asked me if I would like to be hired as an interim assistant professor to teach the children's literature course at Washington State University, Pullman, which is the main campus. I was delighted to be hired to do this, but also understood that it was only an interim position and not a permanent one.

You see, universities do not like to hire their own graduates because they believe it is better to bring in someone from another institution who might have a different perspective on the subject being taught. I understand their reasoning, but after teaching the course for a whole year and receiving wonderful evaluations from the preservice teachers, it was hard to step down from the position. They hired a younger lady who came from the East Coast with new ideas for the course.

I did not stay around to find out if she had wonderful new perspectives, as the chair of the department called me in and offered me a tenure track position to teach literacy courses on one of their branch campuses, WSU Tri-Cities, which was located in Richland, Washington.

When I arrived at WSU Tri-Cities, the chair of the department was already teaching children's literature, so I had several new courses to learn and make my own. I was given the syllabi of previous teachers, but you always want to give it your own twist, so I had more learning to do. Over a period of five years, I developed and taught eight different courses at WSU Tri-Cities. I also wrote and co-wrote several articles in peer-reviewed journals. In addition, I was selected to attend a ten-day conference in Japan, where I presented at several American Educational Research Association (AERA) conferences across the United States and Canada.

I worked very hard and became interested in the accelerated reading program, which was being used extensively in the state. It was a computerized program where students read books at their own reading level and then took a test on the computer to see how much they comprehended the text. I decided that was the area I would research, but I had to find a school that would allow me to do that. I drove to Yakima and visited with a principal there, and he approved of having me do research on the effects of using the accelerated reading program on student achievement. Yakima was a three-hour round trip by car, and I spent many hours driving to and from my research location.

While I was at WSU Tri-Cities, my father died at age ninety-four, and my mother had a stroke a few years later. We had to move her to a nursing home in Spokane, Washington, where she could receive medical care. I decided it would be better for me to live closer to Spokane, so I applied for a job at the University of Idaho in the Curriculum and Education Department. I resigned my assignment as an assistant professor at Washington State University and I was offered a position in the literacy department at the University of Idaho in Moscow, Idaho. The U of I was only eight miles from WSU where I first started, so I was happy to be back in the Palouse country.

I taught a required course in teaching literacy for preservice teachers for ten years in Moscow and then I retired. The chair of the department asked me to come back and teach that course again for their branch campus in Coeur d'Alene, Idaho, as well as at the main campus in Moscow. In 2011, I received the Alumni Award for Excellence in Teaching at the University of Idaho in recognition of my outstanding contribution to the academic development of my students. I relished my years of teaching at the University of Idaho. I had found my home!

CLOCK TOWER AT THE UNIVERSITY OF IDAHO

DEANNA'S PARENTS, BILL AND CLARA PETERSCHICK

PETERSCHICK CHILDREN: RICHARD, DEANNA, JIMMY AND CAROLYN

PART SEVEN

Memorable Stories from the Schoolyard

CHAPTER 32

And So We Begin

As a bonus to the reader, I reached out to my family, friends, and colleagues to write stories to be included in this book because I wanted to honor them. It takes the whole schoolyard to educate a child, not just the teachers. I will start with the story that inspired the title of this book.

I keep in touch with some of my former education students at the University of Idaho, and I invited Macy Swift and Ryann Mata to visit me in Arizona for a few days after school was out. Of course, we talked a lot about teaching and some of the funny things that happened at school. Macy told me a story about her principal at Moscow Charter School and she said, "There was a pig on the playground."

I said, "That would be a great title for my collection of stories from the schoolyard."

From there, I contacted Mr. Tony Bonuccelli, the principal of Moscow Charter School, to write the story for my book and he graciously accepted my offer.

Perceptive Principals: Knock on Wood

By Tony Bonuccelli

It was my first day as the new principal at Moscow Charter School. Of course, I was all decked out in my Sunday finest, with a blue suit and black patent leather shoes. I even wore a red tie.

I started the day with all the students and teachers facing me in an all-school morning meeting. I noticed that the teachers were also dressed in their brightest street clothes. I introduced myself as the new principal, and after a brief meeting I dismissed the teachers and students to their homerooms where they could get to know one another.

As everyone settled in, I sat back in my wooden chair and thought to myself, *It is finally here. My first day as a principal.* I took a deep breath and realized I wanted to see the school in action and enjoy every minute of my first day.

As I headed out of my office on my tour around the school, I walked by the school secretary and commented, "I am not sure what to do. Everything is going so smoothly there's really nothing for me to do."

"You should knock on wood," she responded, and we both laughed.

At that point, I went to see how the classes were moving along. I chose to go to Mrs. Bonzo's fourth-grade classroom because she was a veteran teacher who knew how to organize her students. As I was observing her excellent teaching maneuvers, out of the corner of my eye I saw something run outside by her lower window. I was dumbfounded! It could not be what I thought it was . . .

It was a pig!

Not a big pig, but a little twenty-pound pig. I did a double take and then went to tell the secretary.

"I think there is a pig on the playground."

She replied, "I told you to knock on wood."

We ran to the back door and sure enough, there was a pig lying in the shade under one of the trees on the playground. I had no clue how it had gotten there. I was pretty sure none of the surrounding neighbors had pigs. What worried me was it was about recess time for the elementary students, and if the students ran out on the playground and saw the little pig, they would scream and holler and cause all kinds of chaos.

We called animal control and asked some teachers to help me corral the pig. Since there weren't any nets handy, I had five staff members go out on the playground with poster boards to corner the pig. What a sight that was! The animal control officer arrived and tried to get the noose around his neck, but the little pink pig wasn't having it.

We were all sweating, as it was a ninety-degree day in August, and everyone had their first day attire on, with suits, ties, dresses, and fancy shoes. We ran from one end of the playground to the other madly chasing our pig. He was having the time of his life watching us trying to catch him, snorting gleefully as he easily evaded us . . . Toward the end, the animal control officer said, "Don't let him get off the property."

This made me think, *If it's not on our property, it's not our problem anymore.* At that point, the pig ran into the neighbor's yard. Whew!!!

But our staff, feeling the need to help, ran into the neighbor's yard and helped the animal control officer put the net over its body and then he wrestled it into his pickup and drove away. With the pig finally in custody, I went into my office and sat down. Leaning back in my chair, I said to my secretary, "You can't make this kind of thing up."

She laughed and said, "I told you to knock on wood."

There's no better way to start a day than with bacon, but it's much better when you don't have to wrangle it yourself.

Author Bio: Tony Bonuccelli is the principal of Moscow Charter School in Moscow, Idaho, where he currently resides. He enjoys playing golf with his son and is teaching him how to play the drums. Tony was a band teacher for many years before becoming an elementary principal.

I Relish the Challenge

By Frances Connor

I was the principal at Westside Elementary grades kindergarten through six with almost five hundred students. In the beginning I was excited to be the instructional leader. But it was during my first year there that I got divorced, so I ended up being a single mother. Caroline was just a baby, and at times we had to wait for someone to pick her up to take her to the babysitter, so I strapped her on my back and took her to work with me. I'd wear her on my chest and she became my assistant principal. She is currently a student at that same school.

Things were going great, but my life changed a lot when COVID-19 came along. We had to teach online and it was very hard. Only one teacher left our school after Covid because we were a tight knit group of teachers. After Covid, things returned pretty much to normal.

As a principal, I had a lot of extra duties. One year, I was the recruitment person to try to get teachers to come work for us in the Idaho Falls School District. I loved that part of my job because I would visit different colleges and even go to Wyoming and Oregon to recruit teachers. Wyoming pays their teachers well, so if we got one student from Wyoming, we felt pretty good. We did get many recruits from our own area, because a lot of students from nearby universities and colleges did their practicums and student teaching in our district.

One of my favorite roles as a principal was being a bridge between the teachers and the parents. I would try to calm the parents down and help everyone find a solution to the problem.

I continued as the principal for four years, and at that point in time, I wasn't sure if I ever wanted to get married again, so I concentrated on getting my education specialist master's degree. As I was pursuing that degree, I met Layne Conner and changed my mind about becoming an education specialist.

We hit it off and eventually got married. We had a baby girl named Jolie and I decided to devote more time to my family, so I became an assistant principal at the middle school. There were several assistant principals so I did not have as much power as I did at the elementary school. I talked to Layne about it and he said, "You have your whole life to do this."

I talked to my administrators about it and they tried to convince me to stay, but I decided to go back to the classroom. I was assigned to teach fifth grade at a low-income school across town, and it was my favorite year of teaching. Although I had a difficult class, it was very challenging and very humbling. It sparked my love of education again.

When you are in administration, you get tied into the politics of things. When you have your own classroom you are in charge of what goes on there. I was only there for one year because two of my teacher friends came to me and asked me out for dinner. There, they asked me if I would teach at a new charter school they were opening in the district. It is called Elevate Academy and it is for students who are not finding success in regular schools. There's a few of them in Idaho and the goal is that the students will be certified in two trades by the time they leave high school. Then, they can choose which trade they want to pursue as an occupation.

Layne and I went to Parma to observe their program before I made my decision, and I was very impressed. Not every child is on the college route and this gives them a chance in life.

I was the first teacher they hired and I was able to recruit my own team to work with me. The first year, 2024, we had students from grades six to ten. Eventually they will add grades eleven and twelve. Some of the courses we teach are: construction/welding, culinary arts, criminal justice, firefighting, business/marketing, graphic design, medical arts, and others according to community input and need. It is an exciting time for me because I love teaching middle school and will relish this challenge.

Author Bio: Frances loves teaching middle school students at Elevate Academy. She and her husband Layne enjoy camping, skiing, and doing anything outside with their two daughters, Caroline and Jolie.

Amazing Alaska Teachers: Villagers Know Best

By Tracy Hoffmeister

In 2007-2008, I made the bold move to teach in a small Unangan village of Nikolski, Alaska. Nikloski is on Umnak Island, which is part of the Aleutian Chain near Dutch Harbor. I had never been to Alaska, let alone spent a whole year in an isolated village.

I was the only teacher, teaching all subjects for ten students in ten different grades. I loved teaching the Unangan students; they were teaching me their native language and hanging out with me in my home a lot. We had game nights, bonfires, and anything else we could think of to hang out.

Everything was running smoothly until the village started to run out of diesel fuel, which ran all of the power plants for the island. The elders ordered in a very large load of diesel fuel and the school had an order in, as well.

When the barge came in, the men on the boat decided to tie this huge barge full of fuel up to a D6 tractor. The native people told them it was not a good idea, that winds come up very suddenly with no warning and can be forty to fifty miles per hour.

The men on the barge ignored the native people and tied it up. They had just started unloading some of the fuel and, surprise, surprise, the winds came in. The barge pulled the D6 tractor into the bay and fuel spilt everywhere into the pristine Bering Sea. The barge left and the people on it said that they would not come back.

The village could have received barrels of fuel by plane, but the runway had several feet of snow on it, and it was the time of year that the storms were constant, one right after the other. Since the D6 tractor was in the sea, there was no way to plow the runway.

The situation was getting dire. I did not want to close the school down because we couldn't heat the building. The thing about Umnak Island is that there are no trees on the island. There was a bit of driftwood, but not enough to heat a school, which didn't have a wood-burning stove anyway.

I decided to check the school tank and found out that there was a layer of diesel fuel along the bottom of it that might get us through the rest of the year.

The fuel was so low that the pump wouldn't pump it out any longer, but there was a spigot that could be opened and the fuel dispensed by hand.

My house was right next to the school and had its own fuel tank, so I decided that I would close down the school and have the students meet in my house. The space was much smaller to heat and we should be able to haul enough fuel from the big tank to my smaller tank.

The students were all on board. We got five-gallon buckets and cloth to strain the dredges out of the fuel, filled up the buckets, and hauled them up the hill to my tank. Working together, we were able to outlast the fuel shortage and keep the school open the whole school year.

In the middle of the wait for new fuel, one of my students talked to me right before lunchtime and said that the caribou were close to town and wondered if he could go hunting. The village was running low on food too, so I told him it was a great idea and if he didn't make it back to school that day it was fine.

He was back in an hour. I asked him if he wasn't able to get any caribou and told me he shot two, gutted them, and took them to his mom to hang up to cure. I was dumbfounded; this student was sixteen years old and so competent! I have since heard from him and he is working with all of the native villages on the Aleutian chain to make things better for them.

There was a break in the storms so the villagers decided that if we all worked together, we could hand shovel the runway and get in some food and fuel. The whole village came together, every age, and shoveled the runway. We cleared it well enough to get a plane in to keep the village running until a different barge company would come in who would actually believe that native people know more about their home than inlanders do!

I loved my time in Nikolski, but I was very grateful I could fly off the island when I did because two weeks later, two volcanoes blew and the villagers were stuck again for several months.

I admire the native Unangan people. They are resilient; they have overcome more hardship than you and I can never imagine, yet they are the happiest people I have ever met. I have never laughed so much in my life! I truly am a better person for knowing each and every one of them.

Author Bio: Tracy Hoffmeister lives in Palouse, Washington, and has been teaching at Moscow Charter School for seventeen years. Prior to that, she taught in Colfax, Washington, and Wyoming for several years. She has a black and white cat named Sylvester who she calls her baby. When she was in Nikolski, Alaska, the native people honored her by giving her the native Unangan name of Tiglam Avagaa (Eagle Woman).

The Basket

By Rick Gilmore

The year was 1973, and Alaska had only been named an official state fourteen years before we arrived there to teach for the Bureau of Indian Affairs. My wife and I were assigned to teach in the Yupik village of Tununak, Alaska, located on the Bering Sea. I was the teacher for grades four to eight and my wife, Deanna, was the teacher for grades kindergarten to grade four.

In the middle of my first year of teaching in Tununak, the supervisor of the Bureau of Indian Affairs asked me if I would like to have some of my eighth grade students participate in a cultural exchange with students in the city of Anchorage, Alaska. Five of our students would fly to Anchorage and spend seven days with host families there, and in return, our village would host students from Anchorage for one week. I thought it was a great idea so I lined up host families for the future visit.

The day finally arrived when the five students from Anchorage flew in on a Twin Otter and landed on the dirt runway in the village of Tununak. The whole village turned out to greet them with their best mukluks and parkas on display. I read off the list of names and the host families took them to their homes.

The homes in Tununak were smaller than the homes in Anchorage. They also had no running water or electricity, so no TV. In addition, the students had to use honey buckets, which consisted of a small bucket placed behind a calico curtain, to go to the bathroom. The sleeping quarters consisted of homemade beds with several people sharing the area. Their life was based mostly on subsistence living . . . living off the spring catch of seal, seal oil, and dried herring. The children in the Yupik families found ways to play on the tundra, collect wild berries, and slide in the snow on makeshift cardboard sleds. The Anchorage students would soon realize that the people and children were happy and enjoyed their own way of living.

The visiting students attended classes with students from their host families. I was their teacher and after two days, one of the students from Anchorage came up to me. He was crying and he asked me if he could go home. I told him that he couldn't because it was too expensive to send just one student home. I put my arm over his shoulder and led him back down to his host family. As I walked in the door, the lady of the house was sitting on the flooring sewing a basket. She was using willows she had collected from the tundra and was gently forming a large round receptacle. She would later make a perfectly formed lid to cover the basket. The boy was very curious about this and I suggested to the lady of the house that he might be interested in making a basket and taking it home to his mother. He seemed to like that idea so he sat down beside his host mother and watched her. I left her home and went about my own work at the school.

I didn't hear anything more from the young man from Anchorage during the week. Then it came time for all of the students to return home to Anchorage on the same Twin Otter that brought them to the village. Four of the students eagerly boarded the plane, but one person was unaccounted for. When I was reading off the list of students, I realized the missing student was the boy who had come crying to me to go home. The pilot was waiting, so I quickly went to the host family to look for the boy. I opened the door to the house and there he was sitting on the floor next to his host mother, sewing the last touches on the basket he was going to give to his mother. I told him he could finish the last stitches at his home in Anchorage, but that he had to leave now. He stood up, picked up his unfinished basket and hugged his host mother goodbye. I thought to myself that he had learned more than just schoolwork on his trip to Tununak, Alaska.

Author Bio: Rick Gilmore is a retired US Immigration Inspector and is now living in Moscow, Idaho, with his wife Deanna. They have fourteen grandchildren and fifteen great grandchildren who live in various states. Rick is also the dog whisperer to their two fur babies, Riley and Hazel.

Awesome Agriculture Teacher: There is Joy in Teaching Agriculture

By David Myers

I grew up on a dairy farm in Outlook, near Sunnyside, Washington. I started working at a young age, so farming came naturally to me. Then, when I got older, I worked at a food processing plant and became interested in that aspect of farming. After I graduated from high school in 1956, I decided to attend Washington State University (WSU) and study food processing. When I got there, I found out that they did not have a program for that. I wanted to learn something I was familiar with, so I took classes for teaching agriculture.

After graduating from WSU, I was out with a friend in Sunnyside, Washington, at a burger café. I saw this pretty girl ordering something and I asked, "Who is that?"

My friend answered, "That's Carolyn Howat. She just graduated from high school. Do you want to meet her?"

Of course I said, "Yes."

My friend told me that he would take her on a date and I could meet her then. I had a girlfriend at the time, but when we double-dated that night, Carolyn and I spent most of the time talking to each other. We clicked, and one night I made some excuse to take her home, and after six months of dating, we decided to get married. When I asked her father for her hand in marriage, I told him I would pay for her college from then on. I could do that because I was a first-year agriculture teacher at Palouse, Washington. We got married and Carolyn drove to WSU from Palouse to finish her degree as a speech therapist.

I enjoyed my four years in Palouse, and since I was so close to the university, I went to school in the summers and received my master's degree.

After Palouse, we moved to the west side of the state and I became the ag teacher in Lynden, Washington. I taught there for eight years and Carolyn pursued her career as a speech therapist. We met many new friends while we were in Lynden and enjoyed the community.

After eight years in Lynden, we moved to Poulsbo, Washington, and I was in for a new adventure. I had been used to teaching students who were members of a farming family, but when I moved to Poulsbo, they told me that there weren't too many people farming in that area. The farming enterprise in that part of the country had been reduced to hobby and Christmas tree farms.

The administrators asked me to start a new program involving horticulture, landscaping, and courses the students could take so they could obtain jobs in those areas.

It wasn't too hard to switch to an emphasis on horticulture because many of the agriculture courses at WSU included plant identification, understanding the different types of soils, and what fertilizers were needed for certain plants.

The district wanted the students to learn academics but also be able to apply what they learned in practical ways.

One year, a student asked me if I would teach a course in horse science. She was very interested in horses and knew a lot about them. I checked with administration and they said the state would not authorize the class, but I could teach it as an elective. I had several students sign up and twenty-five or thirty of the students were girls. The student who asked me to teach the course became my assistant and also added her knowledge to the class. I only taught it for one year but I enjoyed this challenge.

Part of my job was to advise the Future Farmers of America (FFA) organization at the club and to prepare them to compete in various activities such as parliamentary procedure, floriculture, and how to judge animals. During my career at North Kitsap, I took four teams to Kansas

City, where we competed in different events at the national contests.

Teaching ag is not without humor. While I was an ag teacher, I often took teams of FFA members to the national convention in Kansas City, Missouri. I was sitting next to another ag teacher on the bus and he started laughing to himself. I asked him, "What is so funny?"

He said, "I was thinking about a test I just gave my class about pigs. One of the questions was, 'What do you call a castrated pig?' and one of the boys in the class gave a funny answer."

"What did the boy write down?" I asked.

"The boy said, 'A sore boar.'"

We both had a chuckle over that one. In case you want to know, the real answer is a barrow.

I became the vocational director for the Kitsap School District for the last eight years of my career. I am happy to say that during my tenure, the enrollment in vocational education classes doubled in size.

In 1976-1977, I was pleased to be selected as the Outstanding Agriculture Teacher of the Year for the state of Washington. Overall, I loved the variety of courses I taught and enjoyed my years as an agriculture teacher.

Author Bio: David divides his time between his condominium in Spokane, Washington, and his cabin on Discovery Bay on the coast. He has three children: Carrie (Ron) Nielsen, and granddaughters Isabella and Emily; Kristin (Mike) Nester and grandchildren Michael and Lucy; David (Karen Ramsahai) Myers and grandchildren, Libby, Lexie, and Levi.

Busy Bus Driver: Sit on your Tuchus!

Louise McNeil

I never thought I would grow up to be a school bus driver, but that is exactly what I did. And I love it! I have been driving school bus for the Deer Park School District in Washington state for over twenty-six years now. How did I get into it?

I was a homemaker and I had two children who were school-aged. I met a lady who was a bus driver for the school district and her mother-in-law was the boss of the bus drivers. She convinced me that I would be able to manage that big bus and possibly enjoy the job. The main thing was that when my children got out of school for vacations and summer break, I would also be off work at the same time. I decided to do it and I never looked back.

My boss was hard, but she had a reason to be strict about our driving. We had children to get to and from their homes in a safe manner. The hardest part about driving a school bus is driving in bad weather. Sometimes the roads are icy and there might be a lot of snow on the road. You just have to know how to slow down and drive in those conditions. In fact, it is easier to maneuver a bus on icy roads than an automobile.

Someone asked me what my schedule was and I told him that I woke up at 5:20 a.m., left the house at 6:10 a.m., and started my bus route at 6:50 a.m. After I dropped the kids off, I went home and returned to the school for my afternoon bus route. I did this for fourteen years, but now I drive a bus for special needs students, and at 10:30 a.m. I take some high school students into Spokane where they take courses at the New Tech Skill Center. I just stay there until they return to Deer Park at 2:30 p.m., and then I take my special students home. I have a paraprofessional who helps me with special needs students. It would be hard to drive the bus and take care of some of the situations that occur there without help, but I love the special needs students. I really like the students who are a little on the sassy side, because they usually tell the other students what to do or not to do.

The younger students sit up in the front close to me and the older students sit in the back. Sometimes, if an older student is acting up, I make him or her come sit in the front with the little kids. There are mirrors in the front and back of the bus so I can monitor what is happening at all times.

The students know I am a little strict and I am always telling them they have to sit on their tuchus. They think that is a funny word, but they know what it means.

One time, a short little boy kept standing up trying to talk to me. I asked him, "Why do you stand up like that?"

He said, "Because I can't see you and it's not polite."

How can you get upset about something like that? But I did tell him, "Well, you have to sit on your tuchus from now on."

Someone once asked me why I didn't become a schoolteacher since I seemed to like the kids so much. I told her that I don't like staying in the classroom all day, and as a bus driver, I get to see the same kids every year and really get to know them. Teachers have to give up their students after one year, but I have known some of mine from kindergarten to high school. Being a bus driver is the best job!

Author Bio: Louise lives in Deer Park with her husband Mike, who is a retired fisherman. They have two married children, Rachel (Kyle) Smith and Kevin (Katie) McNeil. They love to spend time with their five grandchildren and even have bunk beds waiting for any and all of them to visit.

Caring Coaches: Do It Because You Love It!

Annie Christiansen

Annie Christiansen grew up in Gilbert, Arizona, where she played volleyball at Highland High School. Her parents wanted all of their children to play sports because they would be so tired after school that they wouldn't even think about getting into trouble.

Annie made first team All-Conference for the state of Arizona, so she received a scholarship to play volleyball at Yavapai Community College in Prescott for two years. Then, she transferred to Northern Arizona University (NAU) in Flagstaff, where she received another scholarship to play volleyball. While there, the coach wanted the players to put on camps for younger students to raise money for their volleyball team, so she did that. She found out that she was good at teaching younger students how to play volleyball.

At the same time, she wanted to become a nurse, so she took all the courses needed to complete her Bachelor of Science in Nursing. After she graduated from NAU, she got married to her husband Donnie, who became a dentist. They moved to California with the military.

Later on, they moved back to Arizona where she became an oncology nurse. Annie was also coaching volleyball, so the team had to practice from 7:30-9:30 p.m. after she finished her nursing shift.

She then became an emergency room (ER) nurse and it was a lot harder to get in the practices because of her schedule, so she became an assistant coach.

In between all of this, they expanded their family and added three girls and a boy to the mix. One of her daughters was born placenta previa and she weighed only three and a half pounds. It was very hard, but Annie finished the volleyball season with her girls.

Annie thinks that the best part about being a coach is when you teach the players something and they come back from an elite team and say, "I remember when you told me to never pass the ball with one arm. No one else ever told me to do that."

She also says that the hardest part about coaching is working with the parents. For example, a parent might say, "Why doesn't my daughter play more? That girl made seven mistakes and you are still keeping her in." That is just one example of some of the things that parents say.

One of the most exciting things that happened to her is that the team she coached at American Leadership Academy (ALA) Gilbert North won State in 2023. It was the first year the school won, and both of her daughters were on the team so it was extra special to her.

Annie also believes that team sports teach leadership skills and how to get along with others. This is a skill students will need when they become professionals. As a last note, Annie says that if someone is going to be a coach, they should only do it if they love it.

Author Bio: Annie Christiansen lives in Gilbert, Arizona, with her husband Donnie and four children: Kate, Kylie, Blake, and Brooklyn. The family also has a golden doodle named Diesel who is pure joy, no matter what.

You Have to Love Your Content

Rachel Smith

Rachel McNeil grew up in Deer Park, Washington, with her parents Mike and Louise McNeil and her little brother Kevin. She loved doing anything physical and she played three different sports in high school. Basketball was her favorite sport and she was very good at it. When she was a junior in high school, she tore her ACL (anterior cruciate ligament—a ligament in the knee that helps stabilize the knee joint), and she had a wake-up call. She realized that sports might not be forever, so she became interested in the physical aspect of our bodies.

After completing her basketball career at Deer Park High School, Rachel received a full ride scholarship to row at Washington State University in Pullman, Washington. While at WSU she studied kinesiology and loved all of her classes. Her plan was to go into sports medicine . . . then it happened again. While rowing, she tore the ACL in her other knee, and after recuperating from that, a friend asked her to help coach a third-grade volleyball team. Rachel fell in love with her students and with teaching. She decided to switch her major to education, and her goal was to become a K-12 PE teacher and eventually an athletic director. While taking classes, Rachel started refereeing volleyball and basketball games in the area.

Rachel met Kyle Smith while attending WSU, and after completing her student teaching at Mead High School in Spokane, she returned to the Palouse area to be near her boyfriend. Kyle received his master's in mathematics and was hired to teach college courses at St. Martin's College in Lacey. Rachel and Kyle were married and moved to Yelm, Washington, where Rachel became a long-term substitute teacher for the district. She also coached volleyball and track at North Thurston High School. She eventually got a full-time job teaching weight training and PE for the Steilacoom School District. She loved the idea that the students would see her as the weight training teacher, because the job is normally placed in the hands of a male teacher. Rachel loved her job at Steilacoom, but it was a forty-minute drive each way. A PE teaching position opened up closer to her home at North Thurston High School and she has been there ever since. She teaches five classes a day and has between 130 to 140 students. While at North Thurston, Rachel teaches Sports Medicine 1 and 2, and she has a special program where she teaches high school students how to become referees for basketball, volleyball, and baseball games. They can start when they are sixteen and they get paid to referee games. It is a skill that can carry them through their college years.

The advice she would like to give future PE teachers is to make sure you have multiple options. If one sport or class doesn't work out, make sure you are ready to fall back on an alternative. Rachel also suggests that you be confident in who you are and to control what you can control. Rachel likes being a coach and PE teacher because the job helps you relate to your students. You see your students at the different sports events and they are always ready to say hi to their PE teacher and coach. All in all, Rachel loves being a teacher!

Author Bio: Rachel lives with her husband Kyle in Lacey, Washington. They have two daughters, Mackenzie and Morgan, and they love attending sporting events and anything to do with the WSU Cougars and Seahawks football team. The family also loves to play with their Corgi named Oreo.

Creative Cook: I Helped Feed the Future

Gladys Gilbertson

I was raised in Gillette, Wyoming. It was a small city and had around 200,000 people at the time I was growing up there. My father worked in the oil field and was in charge of the propane tanks. I was the youngest of ten children and enjoyed growing up in a smaller city.

After high school, I met my future husband in Gillette. Terry Gilbertson was from Montana and he was working in road construction when I met him. My sister was a flag girl and she was dating another truck driver like Terry. She set me up with him on a double date. Terry and I hit it off, and after dating a few months, we got married at my parent's home in Gillette.

Terry graduated from Flaxville High School in Montana, and his parents had a farm there. After getting married, we moved to the farm in Flaxville and we also lived in Scobey, Montana, for a while. I had three boys over a period of time and we eventually bought a tire shop in Plentywood, Montana. We moved there and all my children graduated from Plentywood High School.

Several years ago, the superintendent of Plentywood Schools asked me if I would like to work at the school as the head cook and kitchen manager. I interviewed for the job and was hired on the spot.

The head cook wanted to step back and let someone else run the kitchen, so she remained as one of my cooks. I ended up working there for twenty years.

I really liked my job, but I had get up early because I was the first one there. I would start the main meal by 6:00 a.m. each day. While I was there, I also started the breakfast program, which went over very well. It was funded by a government grant that allowed us to buy breakfast equipment like large toasters and cereal dispensers. Anyone could have breakfast and it was very inexpensive.

Our kitchen staff served over 400 students a day, as we covered grades kindergarten through seniors in high school. Five people worked for me and they all had different jobs to do every day. For example, one lady worked the salad bar and another person was in charge of doing the dishes.

The school population declined over the years, so we had to drop down to four workers in the kitchen. We were all in charge of cleaning the floors, washing the tables, and setting things up for the next day. There were times I had to spend in my office ordering the food and filling out government forms. One time, one of the officials wanted to tell me which children were on the free and reduced lunch program and I asked him not to tell me. I said, "I don't want to know. To me, they are all equal."

The best part about being the head cook was getting to interact with the students. I tried to make the lunchroom an inviting place, and at Halloween, the girls and I would dress up in costumes. We had a different theme every year. At other times, we just dressed up for fun. One year, all the cooks and servers dressed up like Anne Geddes babies. At other times we had games and gave out prizes for different things. We just wanted to make their meals enjoyable.

There were times I had to discipline some of the students, and if they were rude, they were restricted from coming to the lunchroom for a week or two . . . depending on the severity of their actions.

The students' favorite lunches were pizza and spaghetti. We made the spaghetti from scratch and we boiled over eighty pounds of noodles every time we had it.

I was able to attend special conferences every summer for the head cooks, and since I became one of the senior cooks, I also taught some of the courses.

Being a school cook can be very tiring as you are on your feet for eight to ten hours a day. We got raises every year, but after being the head cook there for twenty years, my top salary was $15 an hour. I think the cooks get paid more than that now; at least I hope so.

I was almost sixty when I retired because I found I wasn't enjoying the job as much as I had when I first started. But isn't that the way it is with most jobs? I hope I improved the lives of the students and teachers while I was there. They had a wonderful retirement party for me and gave me a pin that said, "I helped feed the future."

If I had to do it over, I would do it again in a heartbeat!

Author Bio: Gladys divides her time between her farm in Flaxville, where she lives with her husband Terry and Wahpeton, and North Dakota where two of her sons live. Their oldest son, Clinton, is a professor at North Dakota State College of Science, and their middle son, Wade, teaches social studies and coaches football at Wahpeton High School. Their youngest son, Jeff, and his wife live in Colorado, where he has his own business. Gladys and Terry enjoy visiting and playing with their nine grandchildren and two great grandchildren.

Excellent ESL Teacher: I Want My Life to Count for Something

Sharon Avers

I grew up in Downey, California, with my mom, dad, and two little sisters. I had a wonderful life with my family, and after graduating from high school, I went to Cerritos Community College. I really didn't know what to major in at the time, but my goal was to become a flight attendant. In my day, that appeared to be a glamorous job. I applied, but I was too tall. They had height restrictions at the time and I must have eaten a lot of Wheaties because I grew to be five feet nine inches.

Since I could not become a flight attendant, I decided to take some education courses at California State University, Long Beach. After two years, I received my Bachelor of Arts in elementary education and was hired to teach in the Westminster School District, where I taught for three years. In the interim, I married my husband, Brian Avers, and had two children, Stephen and Lisa. After they were born, I stayed home to raise them.

After several years together, I got divorced and became a single mother. I decided to return to teaching at Westminster Elementary, where I remained for the next twenty-nine years.

In 1975, when Saigon fell to the North Vietnamese, Westminster became the city where many Vietnamese settled. The parents sent their children to Westminster Elementary where I taught. The children could not speak English, so I became an English as a second language (ESL) teacher. It was challenging and new to me, but I loved the children. Vietnamese children did not mess around. They meant business and they were there to learn. The parents were very respectful and sometimes bowed to me. I had no discipline issues.

I was so interested in this field that in 1972 I received my master's degree in teaching English as a second language from Azusa Pacific University.

I have an interesting story to share with you. One year, when I was teaching third grade, a tiny Vietnamese girl named Anh Nguyen came to my classroom. Her coat was too big for her, but she was eager to learn English. I taught her English vocabulary words using cards and concrete objects. I also used total body response techniques to teach her such things as, 'sit down' and 'stand up.' Anh learned very quickly, and at the end of the year went on her way.

I didn't think about her too much until one year I attended an ESL teacher's conference at a fancy hotel. I was seated with people I did not know. Then the announcer introduced a panel of high school students and asked them to talk about the teachers who taught them English.

I didn't recognize her, but my former student stood up and said, "My name is Anh Nguyen and the teacher who taught me English was Sharon Avers. She was wonderful, patient, and kind, and I owe a lot to her."

The other teachers who were sitting at my banquet table saw my name tag and said, "That's you! Stand up and be recognized."

I did and I received a round of applause and a look of wonder from my former student. We talked after the program and kept in touch by writing letters to each other. It was a validating experience for me.

One of the cutest things that happened to me as an ESL teacher was when a small girl with two pigtails named Binh Tram walked up to my desk. She handed me a note she had written. I opened it and it said, "Mrs. Avers. Please do not be absent on Friday, May 10. Our class is having a surprise birthday party for you. Please wear your best dress. Your student, Binh Tram."

I saved that letter over the years, and if you want to know I never regretted one day being a teacher. Teachers affect the future, and if you teach a child to read, your influence goes on forever. I wanted my life to count for something, and I achieved that by being a teacher.

Author Bio: Sharon lives in Huntington Beach, California. She enjoys visits from her children Steve and Lisa and her grandchildren. She was a travel agent as well as a teacher and has visited six continents. Her favorite place to visit was Israel and the Holy Land.

Helpful Homeschool Teacher: Do You Really Love Kids?

Tara Young

Tara Young has been a teacher for twenty-two years. One of her friends asked her, "What question would you ask someone if they wanted to pursue a career in education?"

She responded, "I would ask that person, 'Do you really love kids?' Because being a teacher is not all that financially rewarding. It takes a lot of energy and hard work to be a teacher, and if you are in it for the money, the money is not there."

Tara should know what she is talking about because she has been a public school teacher, a private school teacher, a homeschool teacher, and a substitute teacher. Her first teaching job was at Trinity Lutheran School in Bend, Oregon. She was a full-time teacher for two years and a three-fourths time teacher for another two years. Then she and her husband Brian moved to Julietta, Nebraska, and she taught English and art for four years at Christ Lutheran School. Her husband was the principal there.

Brian decided to become a full-time speaker for Creationism, and he traveled to different churches to speak on that subject. Their three older children continued to attend Christ Lutheran, but when their fourth child was born, it was a little girl and Tara wanted someone to stay home and play with the baby. She decided to pull all the children from the private school and said to herself, *I am a teacher. I can do this. I can homeschool my children.*

And she has been homeschooling her children for the last twenty-two years. A friend asked her why she started homeschooling, and she said, "I wanted to have someone play with the baby."

And the older children did do that and they became very close to each other. They played together a lot and started singing and harmonizing together. They were often asked to sing in churches for weddings and at the county fair.

Tara started using a Christian curriculum, but over the years she realized she had become an eclectic teacher, using parts of one curriculum over another. She said that each child was different, so they had different needs. They would meet on Mondays when she passed out a folder with all their work inside. They would have all week to finish their work, and she didn't care when they did it as long as it was finished by the next Monday morning. If they procrastinated and did not get it done, they might be grounded from something they wished to do that week. As they got older, Tara felt that she was lacking in some of the math skills they needed to learn on the high school level, so she sent them to the community college in Hastings for some of those courses.

Tara feels that it is a myth that homeschool students don't know how to socialize with others. In her area, there were many homeschools and they met once a week to do special things together like cooking or going on a field trip. Her children also met and worked with children their own age at their local church in Hastings, Nebraska. They even got involved in sports through the local homeschool co-op. One time, the children were involved with too many outside activities and they had to pull back so they could do their academic work.

Something must have worked at her homeschool, as her oldest son Noah, received a BA in marketing from the University of Nebraska and her oldest daughter Eden received a 4.0 for her all her college courses at the University of Nebraska and is now a fourth grade teacher in Texas. Josiah volunteered at the fire department in Hastings when he was seventeen and the Hastings Fire Department helped pay for his training to become a certified paramedic and firefighter. He is currently employed there and lives in Hastings with his wife Abby and their three little girls. Tara's youngest daughter, Selah, is attending Hastings Community College where she is seeking a degree in marketing. Noah worked for a seed company but has become a full-time influencer on TikTok and YouTube and is able to provide for his wife, Sierra, and family of four by advertising for large companies on those platforms. His call sign is The Shiloh Farm.

Author Bio: Tara lives with her husband Brian and daughter Selah. Her three older children all married people they knew from the homeschool co-op. Tara is also a substitute teacher in a local public school. She says that public schools and home schools can all be good. It all depends on the school and the teachers within. All of her grandchildren live in Nebraska, and so she gets to be a grandma to them. Brian and Tara have a unique pet. It is a kangaroo named Bindi and she is one of their favorite pets.

Heroic High School Teacher: Focus on the Students

Gerald Dalebout

I grew up in the small town of Priest River, Idaho. I was the first person in my family to attend college. Wanting to have a unique and rewarding college experience, I attended the University of Idaho, where I received my BA in education. I stayed in Moscow after I graduated and started my teaching career at Paradise Creek Regional High School. It was an alternative high school for students struggling in the regular public high school. I saw an opening to teach English at Moscow High School, so I applied for the job. I was hired to teach English for the ninth, tenth, and eleventh grades. I have been there for thirteen years now and I enjoy my work there.

The first year I taught English at the high school was a little rough. It was hard to motivate the kids because the students I taught either had a low level of reading ability or just didn't like English in general.

On top of that, I came in a little too hot and somewhat of a know-it-all the first year I taught. One of the older teachers, Mr. Ashbourne, took me aside and told me what I was doing and to back off a little. I really listened to him and I appreciated the fact that he told me that about myself. I also had some other mentors who I watched teach and they helped me a lot.

While I was teaching English, there was an opening for a social studies teacher and I jumped at the chance to teach high school social studies and history. Since I was a social studies major, it was natural for me to go in that direction, and I have been teaching history and social studies at Moscow High School for several years now.

When I am teaching, I tend to focus on skill-building and how we can build skills to last for the rest of our lives. Because of this emphasis, I wanted to have the students learn more about our political system in America. Therefore, I started a unit called, 'Let's Play Politics,' where the students participate in a mock political campaign. This helps them understand how our government works. Also, the freshman class has a project where they read about a historical figure and do a presentation about that person using videos. They share their videos with the students, their parents, and friends.

I guess I might be doing something right as a teacher, because I have been selected to be the Moscow High School Teacher of the Year and the Moscow High School commencement speaker for two years. These honors are all voted on by the students, which I really appreciate. In 2021, the Idaho Board of Education gave me the Master Educator Award.

In 2020, I was selected for a Fulbright Scholarship award, and my wife Katie, our three sons, and I packed up to go to the Netherlands for six months so I could study their assessment system. Right when I was in the thick of things Covid started, and after ten weeks, we were shipped back to the States so I did not get to complete my research project.

Someone asked me what advice I would give to people wanting to be a teacher, and I said, "Two things are important. First, focus on the students, and second, set boundaries for yourself. Don't take on too many things that you are asked to do, as you can get burned out that way. Try to have a balance between your family life and work life."

I suggest that you watch other people teach and learn what they do to discipline students and do what they do. I also read books about teaching and I would like to give a shout-out to a book titled *Teach Like a Champion*, that was written by Doug Lemov and published in 2021. It is a very helpful book for high school teachers. I read almost everything he writes and follow some of the guidelines presented by real teachers.

Most of all, I think you should love the kids and love teaching. If you do this, you will be on your way to becoming an excellent teacher.

Author Bio: Gerald is married to his high school sweetheart Kate and he said that he might have been in jail or dead without her in his life. They have three sons: Liam, Finn, and Milo. Gerald and Kate also have a large bernadoodle named George, and Gerald says that George is his best friend.

Lovable Librarian: Teachers Don't Do It for the Money

By Debbie McNeil

I graduated from Washington State University in 1977 with a BA in education and a K-nine teaching certificate. My first job was teaching fifth grade in St. Maries, Idaho. I loved my students there, but the next summer I married my husband, Jack McGrath, and since he was already teaching in Pullman, Washington, I got a full-time job teaching fifth grade at Sunnyside Elementary in the same city.

I was happy there, but the Pullman School District closed one of their middle schools and they had too many teachers in the district. Since I was one of the last teachers hired, they had to let me go because of a reduction in force (RIF). There's a saying that fits this description, "Last one hired, first one fired."

Luckily, one of the fifth-grade teachers thought she would try teaching middle school and she decided she did not like it. Therefore, I was hired to be the full-time sixth-, seventh-, and eighth-grade teacher at Lincoln Middle School, and I stayed there for twenty-two years.

While teaching at Lincoln Middle School, I continued my education and received my master's degree in integrated curriculum. Later, I studied library science and received a certificate in that area.

After the librarian left the middle school, I became the librarian there for six years. Being a certified teacher, I concentrated on teaching research in the library. Then, the principal had to cut some staff and told me I had several options for staying in the district. He said, "Let's send you to the high school and see what you like up there."

I visited a couple of the English classes and I fell in love with the kids. I didn't want to take the librarian's job away from her at the high school, so I decided to be a high school teacher.

I taught world history. Then, the following year, President Bush's "No Child Left Behind" program said that we had to be 'highly qualified' in our field. I was short five points from being 'highly qualified,' so they had to send a letter out to the parents saying, "Ms. McNeil is not 'highly qualified' to teach Social Studies."

It was kind of embarrassing, but it wasn't just me, it was other teachers too. It was a hard time for teachers.

I was at the high school for fifteen years. It seemed that most of the teachers didn't want to teach ninth grade English, so at one point

I said I would teach ninth grade English and that is what I ended up doing for my last few years of teaching.

I liked the high school students because they were enthusiastic and inquisitive, and they were also pretty funny, too. The most rewarding part of teaching is working with people who do not have a set way of looking at the world.

I had students in guided practice and study, and they were kids who were behind in their schoolwork. I tried to help them figure out the easiest way to get the results they needed in the least amount of time. I used to say, "Let your brain sweat on this."

Sometimes they wanted to take the easy way out, but I wanted them to realize that they could be lifelong learners. One year, I received an award from Washington State for "Educating the Whole Child." I think I got that award because I watched out for those kids. I might pay for someone's lunch and I tried to find different ways to help them be successful as opposed to *this is the way you do it.*

If you ask me, I would say that the majority of teachers don't do it for the money. I would also tell teachers to teach for five to seven years before they decide to stay or quit the profession. Research shows that if you can make it through seven years, you will make a career out of it.

I would tell them to listen to the older teachers. You might not agree with everything they say, but they can give you some ideas about how to do things at school. If you can find an older teacher who will listen to you and your ideas as much as you will listen to their ideas, that's a good one.

Author Bio: Debbie McNeil lives in Pullman with her husband, Jack McGrath, who was also a teacher in the Pullman School District. They visit their grandchildren in Boise, Idaho, and have six tabby cats at home. One of them, named Homer, sits on Debbie's lap when she is working on the computer. Debbie still quilts and is a master gardener for the State of Washington.

Marvelous Middle School Teachers: The Power of . . . Just Being There

By Paul Collins

There's very little worse than teen angst. Wait . . . pre-teen angst. That's definitely worse. I say this because at least teenagers, the high schoolers, have VALID reasons for that angst. Relationships, part-time jobs, picking a college—heck, even trying to decide to go to college!—and navigating trying to become an adult when they know they know way more than their mom and dad but they still have to obey rules in order to get the keys to the car. Phhhfff . . . what do parents know anyway?!

The pre-teens, the middle schoolers . . . ugh, what a train wreck their anxious little bodies are. Their bodies are literally betraying them. Body odor they didn't sign up for . . . plugged pores on their faces they have no idea how to deal with . . . even their very vocal cords rise up in a discordant ear-piercing crackling cacophony. The drama they experience, they live, and they spread around like muddy footprints after a thunderstorm. They *are* that thunderstorm. It's enough to drive even the most patient of adults to their wits end. But at the end of the day, those ten-, eleven-, twelve-, and thirteen-year-olds still know that Mom's gonna have dinner on the table, Dad's still going show up at their baseball or soccer game, Grandma's still going to pinch their cheeks, and their aunts and uncles are still going to show up for their unicorn princess cupcakes or G.I. Joe-themed birthday party. There is a good chance they still have a teddy bear or other 'stuffy' sitting on their bed. They still have somebody to do their laundry for them, pay for that new video game they simply *must* have, and be the safety net that they still ABSOLUTELY must have.

Now, don't get me wrong. I'm not trivializing their trials and tribulations. There ARE serious issues that are being dumped on their shoulders. This is a generation the planet has never seen before. Tik Tok videos, Instagram posts, vines, and viral feeds are distorting their view, their perception, and the very nature of their world, their society, and their journey to adulthood. This is a generation totally unprepared for what society is dumping on them because no other generation has had to deal with this kind of a crapfest before. Their parents don't know how to help them because smartphones didn't exist when they were kids, and their friends are just as confused, bewildered, and desperate for help as they are, and teachers are doing the best they can to simply convince them that math is useful . . . and that not everybody is going to grow up to be a YouTube star. Be quiet slime-making-kid, I know you're already make more money than I do! Not everybody is that lucky.

So what do kids need now? What kind of Superman or Wonder Woman hero can they find to save the day? None. There isn't one. Superheroes don't exist. Hogwarts letters aren't ever coming. Those things aren't even needed.

What kids do need is someone who will simply . . . be there. To have an adult who knows when to shut up and sit down; to let the kid talk through their angst (even if it's as ridiculous as the kid dropping their coconut-skim-steamer-with-extra-foam-and-rainbow-sprinkles on the sidewalk). Oh look . . . their BFF caught it on video and is now posting in on Snapchat. Super.

There's an unbelievable power in just . . . being there. To stand there and listen, to let a trust be built between you and them. Just being there; to stand there and to let it quietly show them that you are a trusted adult. That no matter what is happening in their life, you'll be there to help them out. That's a power most adults forget about. That's something that these kids NEED. They don't need a teacher to yell and shout about how they aren't applying themselves. They don't need guilt trips about how disappointing their actions are. They NEED to be held accountable for their actions! I'm not in any way saying to coddle them and 'protect' them from the consequences they earned. But what they need is someone who is going to help see them through the mess they made. Someone who will be there; a metaphorical hand to cling to in the hurricane of their lives, a lighthouse to give them enough light to know that the storm will end. What that girl, whose father is borderline abusive, needs is someone to show them that they're gonna make it. The boy who was abandoned by his mother, dad's in prison, and lives with his chain-smoking grandma who only screams at him, needs the exact same thing. Someone to remind them to take it one day at a time. To simply stand there and show them that when they make it for twenty-four hours that it's one day down and another to go. And after the next twenty-four hours pass, that's another day down. Another day to prove that they are still there. That they made it. That they're gonna be okay.

Sometimes just being there WON'T be enough. Sometimes kids need more than the teacher, the counselor, the positive adult can give. We're not Superman or Wonder Woman. We can't always save the day. We can't always save them all. No one on this planet can. But we can show up. We can just . . . be there for them.

Author Bio: Paul has been teaching middle school for twelve years. His side hustle is as a nature and rural photographer. He and his husband are actively working on fulfilling their dream of having their own little piece of Palouse Paradise, which will be filled with trees, native prairie plants, and a pond to bring in the wild animals, to be photographed, of course.

Not All Teachers Like to Teach Middle School Students

By Ryann Mata

Ryann grew up in Boise, Idaho, in a family that consisted of a mom, dad, one brother, and two sisters. She was the oldest child, so sometimes she would babysit her younger siblings. What did they do for fun? Play school, of course, where Ryann would always play the teacher role.

Both her mother and grandmother were teachers who both graduated from the University of Idaho.

Ryann decided to attend the University of Idaho, as well. She majored in biology, thinking she might do something in that field. She also took some education classes while she was there, and one time, she was assigned to do a practicum at Moscow Charter School. She found out she loved teaching, and while she was there, an opening came up to teach mathematics in the middle school. She was strong in the area of math and had taken many advanced placement classes in high school, where she had excelled as a student. She decided to take the job.

While teaching middle school students, she talked to other teachers and found out that not all teachers love to teach middle school students because they are transitioning from being a child to becoming an adolescent. But Ryann found out that she loved the middle school students. She was offered other jobs in the elementary but decided to stick with the middle schoolers and teach math.

She stayed at Moscow Charter School for six years. While there, she taught robotics, which had already been established by a former teacher. She was the STEM teacher, which stands for science, technology, engineering, and math. The idea behind STEM is to have girls become more involved in fields that have traditionally been dominated by boys and perhaps find their own jobs in these areas.

Ms. Mata, as she is addressed at school, took many students on robotics teams to state competitions. Their teams also included what some schools call STEAM, which includes art, drawing, and engineering design. She took three to four teams a year and chaperoned them while competing in robotics competitions. One year, her team won first place at State and was dubbed the Rising All-Stars.

Ms. Mata held her robotics teams practices on Saturdays, which she enjoyed because she got to interact with the students when they were out of school. She and the teams had T-shirts made representing their team logos. One team of five girls made matching chicken outfits and called themselves Cyberchicks. The boys chose Thundercats for their theme and had T-shirts made representing their logo. One team was innovative and called their group the Cyborg Capybaras.

One of Ms. Mata's goals is to receive her master's degree in mathematics and work on the state level to develop new math curriculum for the students. After six years at Moscow Charter School, Ryann moved to Boise, Idaho, to be closer to her family. She is currently teaching middle school mathematics in the Boise School District.

Author Bio: Ryann is now teaching mathematics at Lowell Scott Middle School in the West Ada School District in Meridian, Idaho. She has a significant other named Acer and they enjoy hiking, paddleboarding, camping, and swimming. She enjoys being closer to her large family, who live in Boise.

From One Teacher to Another

By Macy Swift

Even before I entered high school, I heard stories about her: the hilarious yet hard-grading English teacher Mrs. Brown.

"Mrs. Brown? You'll never get an A in her class," kids said, "She's the hardest grader ever! But she does the craziest, fun things and our class loves to prank her!"

I remember the first assignment I got back and the score I got on it: an 8.5 out of 10. Here was someone who was going to make little-old-miss-A-plus-me work for my grades! And work I did.

Whether approved by the modern educational mindset or not, Mrs. Brown's teaching philosophy was "Set the bar high and the cream will rise." She also did not believe in selective grading: she graded every comma, every capitalization error, every misspelling, every time.

But at the same time, Mrs. Brown was the most fun, most ridiculous, most caring teacher you could ever have. And little did I know it, but fifteen-year-old me would go on to have a twenty-year friendship with this crazy yet caring lady.

I have many stories of my time in Mrs. Brown's classroom. I remember what must have been Halloween when she was standing on a stool in front of the class, in a black Zorro costume and mask, performing some antic or another. I remember how the boys would prank her and she would laugh her head off about how loud she had screamed when she had reached her hand in the drawer and touched the piece of moleskin they'd placed there to make her think it was a mouse! I remember her saying, "Let's just go out in the parking lot and play hide-and-seek in and among our cars!" and off we went.

I remember her lowering her voice to a whisper and letting us in on a secret she didn't want the other teachers to know she'd come into the school over the weekend to sneakily use the school ladder to tape over the AC vents in her room and had inadvertently set the fire alarm off! The heating/cooling system wasn't the greatest, and the rooms were often either too hot or too cold. She wasn't technically supposed to be taping over vents, but she did it and escaped before the fire trucks arrived and she was found out.

Despite what students bemoaned as harsh grading, I also remember how clearly she expressed her interest in each student, no matter what grade they got in her class. "Mrs. Brown is so nice," I overheard a senior girl say one time, "She has tears in her eyes when she tells you that you failed her class."

Full of energy, she would enthusiastically respond to anything you shared with her about your life. "Wow! Oh my gosh!" she'd say, and snag anyone passing by to tell them, "Listen to this! Did you hear what happened? Tell them!"

She'd act like she had nowhere else in the world to go and just listen and listen and listen to you after class until YOU had to be the one to excuse yourself and go home. Even the kids who were annoying or poor students in class would still stay after to tell her about their lives. And you could tell that she liked them, even if they weren't good students. I remember she had what she called her "favorite student chair," right up front by her teaching spot. If someone was consistently off-task or distracting others, she'd crook her finger at them, smile, and say, "Aw, come up here to my favorite student chair. This chair is just for you because I like you so much."

And she'd laugh knowingly, as we all would, since that student was certainly not 'the favorite' at that moment, but the concept was conveyed that your misbehavior didn't make her mad at you; you were still "her favorite."

After three years with Mrs. Brown as my English teacher, I graduated from high school and went on to college, majoring in elementary education and Spanish. My younger siblings still attended the high school I had graduated from, so I kept in touch with Mrs. Brown through the grapevine, and when I graduated from college, my high school just so happened to have an opening for a ninth-grade English and Spanish teacher. My previous teachers called and asked me to apply. Even though my certificate was K-8, I landed the job.

"Mrs. Brown" now became "Sharon" to me; my co-worker, teacher mentor, and encourager. I learned that she was just as eager to stand in the hallway and talk and listen for time ad infinitum with us other teachers as she had been with students. Hilarious stories came from that time, such as the time she and the other Spanish teacher tried to rescue me from a parent-teacher conference gone awry and ended up literally hiding behind a bookcase from the psycho parent; the time that students hid a walkie-talkie inside a giant stuffed bear in her classroom and talked to her through the bear from an adjoining classroom as a prank; the time she and I hurriedly sorted through school recycle bins to find a student's graded test that an over-the-top parent literally wanted to dumpster-dive for to see the score.

In the midst of the good memories, though, I was also dealing with serious health complications and making it through the day at work was a challenge. At the end of my second year of teaching, I needed to go on an indefinite medical leave. Sharon was just at the point of retirement, having announced it was her last year in the classroom. Yet, when I could no longer teach, she signed back on at the school as my long-term substitute teacher. "This is Macy's job," she asserted, "and I am going to be a placeholder for her until she can have it back."

As a substitute, she continued to have hilarious times with the students, and despite my many thanks to her, she'd always say, "Oh, this is the best thing ever. I can ease out of teaching this way without having to quit all at once. I'm just a sub now, so I don't have to go to staff meetings or do all the other responsibilities."

She loved her role so much that in the space where my name was over the door, she pasted a paper title for herself: "Just a sub."

Sharon was 'just a sub' for me for two years, phasing out and back in as my health ebbed and flowed. In the end, I was unable to return to teaching for a number of years and Sharon retired, but we stayed in touch. We shared a faith as well as a calling as teachers, and she would often pray for me and my health struggles over the years.

When the time came when for me to return to the classroom, Sharon was, of course, listed as one of my references. Apparently, when she was called for a reference she said, "You better hire this girl or you'll regret it."

When I was offered the job, I was told, "Oh, and your reference Sharon said to say 'hi' to you."

Now in my fourth year of teaching middle school in my new position, I still see the ways Sharon Brown has shaped me as an educator. Although we have different personalities and teaching styles, I still catch myself using classroom strategies I learned from her.

For example, I have 'favorite students' as well, and even a 'favorite student stool' at the front of the classroom for students who are especially off-task that day. I smile and say with a wink, "C'mon, my favorite student. Come sit up here right by me, because I like you so much."

And I remember what it was like to feel like you were the center of her whole world whenever you told her something mundane about your life. When students stop by my desk, I try to stop whatever I am doing, look them in the eye, and give them my complete, rapt attention. I can't always listen forever like Mrs. Brown somehow could, but I try to remember that people are more important than tasks and take the time to tell them, "I love hearing from you and you are really important to me. I wish I could talk all day, but I am going to have to do lesson plans now."

I think the main thing I saw put into practice by Sharon Brown was that each person is special and important, no matter what type of student they are or what grade they earn in the classroom. After all, we teach inside a specific type of school system in a certain country during a certain time period. What happens to be the measure of 'success' in this modern-day school system can change over the years and is even different from what it considered 'success' in other countries. But human value and worth—that doesn't change. And THAT is what is MOST important in the classroom, even if students never do learn how to write a perfect five-paragraph essay.

This last summer, I ended up with a free few days back near my hometown. Having lived inland in Idaho for the past six years, I was dying to go to the coast. But who to go with? Who was fun to be around and up for last-minute adventures? Sharon! I rang her up and in no time we had our beach trip planned. While eating seafood and walking on the beach, we reminisced about teaching—her stories from her early teaching career, stories from times when I was her student and times when I was her co-worker, and my current stories in the classroom. She gave me advice, promised to pray for my difficult students, but most of all we laughed, one teacher with another. I think one of the best outcomes of Mrs. Brown's approach was that by valuing people over performance, she turned students into friends.

My friends and family chuckled a little when I told them I went on a beach trip with my former high school English teacher. My sister said, "Maybe in fifteen or twenty years, *you'll* be going to the beach with one of *your* current students!"

I sure hope so. Thanks to Mrs. Brown's influence, I realize that I make twenty-two new friends each school year–they just happen to be my students for a few years first! And maybe one of them will be MY younger English teacher friend and I'll get to be the "Mrs. Brown" for them.

Author Bio: Macy lives in Moscow, Idaho, and teaches language arts to the middle school students at Moscow Charter School. Macy is working on her master's degree, specializing in dyslexia and reading disabilities.

Magnificent Maintenance Man: Sign Up for the Long Haul

Kelly Pederson

Kelly grew up in Eastern Montana in the small town of Plentywood near the Canadian border. He attended all twelve years of school at Plentywood, where he was involved with the track team. After graduating from high school, Kelly decided to attend a vocational technical (vo-tech) college in Billings, where he learned how to be a mechanic.

He returned to his hometown of Plentywood and was hired as a custodian on March 15, 1979. He worked the night shift for nine years and then was hired as the head maintenance man for the Plentywood School District. He kept this job for thirty-five years, and one of his big responsibilities was making sure the boilers were working in the steam plant. Sometimes, he had to work overtime or on the weekends to make sure the students and teachers had a warm building to come to on a Monday morning. It gets very cold in Plentywood, Montana, during the winters, sometimes as low as minus forty degrees Fahrenheit. Kelly maintains that the hardest part of his job was making emergency repairs on very old steam lines because he had to crawl under tunnels to fix them.

The most rewarding part of his job was getting the football field ready for a new season by mowing the lawn and painting the markers. He also enjoyed refinishing the gym floor to get it ready for a new season of basketball. Although both of these were very big and tedious jobs, he felt a sense of accomplishment in completing them.

Kelly recommends that if a person is interested in doing this job, they should sign up for the long haul, because the benefits and retirement options are very good.

After retiring from the Plentywood School District, Kelly was hired by the City of Plentywood to take care of the parks and the ball fields. He volunteers some of his own time to help out at fast pitch and softball tournaments on the weekends because he said Plentywood people always step up to do the right thing and he feels it is his responsibility to do the same thing.

Author Bio: Kelly currently lives in Plentywood, Montana, but visits his daughter and three grandchildren in Billings to watch their games. They call him Papa Kelly, and when they visit he likes to show them what it is like to live and play in the small town of Plentywood.

Optimistic Online Teacher: Err on the side of the Child

Debbie Stein Savino

I grew up in New Jersey with four siblings. My father was Jewish and my mother was raised Catholic. She converted to Judaism when she married my father. Almost everyone in my neighborhood had come from other countries, so that taught me a lot about diversity and the richness of other cultures.

After graduating from a two-year junior college, I wanted to become a minister, so I continued my education at a Bible college. After graduation, I got married and began a small church in our home. While I loved being in ministry, I soon came to believe my calling was to stay home and take care of my husband and children. I began homeschooling my children, which I enjoyed tremendously.

After twelve years of marriage, I discovered my husband was leading a double life and shortly after became a single mother with seven children. I started a couple of businesses and eventually had to put my kids in public school. At this point I became a paraprofessional in an alternative education program. I realized that if I became a teacher, I could still be home when my kids were home and be able to support my family, so I returned to college to get my master's in teaching degree from Washington State University, Tri-Cities, Washington.

After teaching middle school math for seventeen years, we were told on a Friday we would be out of school for a week due to a virus spreading like wildfire, which was COVID-19, and told not to contact parents or students. I trusted my instincts and took the document camera and a standing whiteboard home with me. I had been taking online courses in teaching personal finance for the previous four years, so I knew I could keep my students learning for however long we would be out.

Contrary to the rules, I contacted my students and told them how to join me on Zoom. I taught pre-algebra and algebra classes five hours a day, five days a week, and my classes were well attended. Some of the parents wrote and said, "How come no one else is doing this? Thank you for making my son get out of bed and brush his teeth this morning."

Or "Thank you for having my daughter get dressed up for the day to attend your Zoom class."

I almost got written up for being insubordinate for doing this, but I did not care. I knew I was serving my students and their families the absolute best I could.

Now, I teach personal finance classes online at our district's alternative online academy, and I wake up every morning knowing I am changing the trajectory of my students' lives!

One incident stands out in my mind that demonstrates how we affect our students. A younger girl came to my class and sat in the back. She looked like she was not paying attention to anything I was teaching and she never participated in class.

One day, she walked up to my desk and pulled something from her sweatshirt. She said, "I got my earbuds."

I asked her, "How did you do that?"

"Duh," she said. "Just like you told me. Y=mx+b!"

I had been teaching about making short-term goals on our 'Financial Fridays' in our algebra class. This brought me to tears and it still does to this day. That was ten years ago.

My advice for new teachers is to stay true to yourself. You should not be afraid to stand up for your values and you need to find another assignment if the one you are in is killing your spirit. Also, be humble with your students. If you accuse them of doing something wrong and they did not commit the offense, they will always remember how you made them feel. If you are not sure about a situation, always err on the side of the child.

My biggest advice is to love them and let them know you care about them. When I taught in person, I used to greet each child with a handshake when they entered my class and said, "I love you and am glad that you are here."

If they had a game the night before, I might ask, "How did your game go?" or "How was your recital?"

Some of the students were too shy to shake hands, so I told them they at least had to make eye contact with me when I greeted them.

We never know what kind of an impact we can make in the life of a child, but we need to try our best to make their lives better in some way.

Author Bio: Debbie lives in Richland, Washington, where she continues to teach online classes. She has eight grandchildren, and most of her children live in the Richland area. She continues to advocate for classes in personal finance and she loves to hike Badger Mountain.

Sensational Teacher and Substitute: On Becoming a Teacher

By Kenneth Paulson

Like the author of *There's a Pig on the Playground*, I also went to Plaza Grade School. In fact, I am Deanna Gilmore's third cousin. Our grandparents were brother and sister before begetting to others.

Like she mentioned, it was an honor to get to play Kick the Can with the older kids. A great reward was being able to clean the chalkboard erasers by pounding them outside on the bricks of the school. Depending on your partner, sometimes it was hard to tell which got the most chalk dust: the eraser or each other. I was in the largest class of seven. Most grades had two to four students. One grade had none.

Learning to play basketball was a real challenge. There was a small basketball court in the cement basement of the school, so you learned to shoot the ball with very little arch because it would hit the low ceiling.

In the fifth grade, I moved to Rosalia Grade School because Plaza Grade School was being consolidated with either Spangle or Rosalia School District. My parents chose to have me go to school in Rosalia. After graduating from Rosalia High School in 1964, I attended Whitworth College in Spokane and earned a degree in education. I began teaching in 1968 in the East Valley School District. After fifty-five years in education (thirty in the elementary classroom and twenty-five as a substitute) I have many fond memories. Some of the best stories are probably the ones that should not be in print.

I do remember the day I was teaching a lesson and I noticed Johnny was missing from his desk. I asked the class if anyone knew where he was. They said, "Oh, Johnny got sick and left the room."

I went back to his desk and he had thrown up all over his book and the top of the desk. The principal came and put the sawdust powder all over the book and desk and all went in the garbage. This was the beginning of my yearly ritual of telling the class, "If you think you might be getting sick, don't wait for permission, and just get out the door. *Then it becomes the janitor's problem.*"

Early in my career, I had a student teacher. It was like having another student in the room, as Bob took a while to grow up. He was always good for a big mess. One day I left for about an hour, and when I returned, the principal met me at the door. It was a nice warm spring day and my student teacher had opened the door in the locker room that goes outside. Bob and my class were having a water fight with buckets. The locker room, Bob, and the kids were all quite wet!

Bob introduced my class to candle making, where they ruined my wife's pot and created a big mess. Every time she tries to use the pot and finds that it is warped on the bottom, she reminds me of this. He also brought in potter's wheels. Needless to say, another big mess!

Bob was from out of town and needed a place to stay. We had an extra bedroom in the basement so we offered to have him stay with us.

We lived in a split-entry house, and one day my wife saw something flash up past the window. Not being sure what it was, I went outside to check it out. He was tossing our young children in the air as high as the window. They thought it was great fun. Their parents . . . *Not So Much!*

One night, my wife heard a strange noise coming from his room, and not feeling good about going in, she woke me up to check it out. Upon investigating, I found Bob sleeping with a hairdryer running underneath the covers. He said he was cold! The second time it happened, I said, "Bob, No more hairdryer. Just turn up the thermostat."

He received his teaching degree and became a physical education teacher on the coast. He developed a traveling program of miniature bicycles and unicycles. Everybody loved Bob, especially the kids. He had some great ideas that he just needed time to perfect. We kept in contact with him over the years when we traveled to the other side of the state of Washington. Last time we saw him was at our daughter's wedding and my retirement party. He has since retired as well and moved back to the small town he lived in as a kid.

Author Bio: Kenneth and his wife Vada have been married for over fifty years. They live in the Spokane Valley. They have a son who farms in Sandy, Oregon, and their daughter and husband live in the Spokane Valley. Her daughter had triplets and Ken and Vada helped babysit them when they were little. The triplets are now twenty-four years old. Ken's hobbies are Sudoku puzzles, reading, and attending Spokane Chiefs' hockey games.

Serious School Secretary: Never a Dull Moment

By Judy Brown

Judy was raised in the small town of Prairie Rose, North Dakota. She always loved school, and even though her graduating class had only thirteen students, she was privileged to be selected as the valedictorian of her class. She remembers giving the speech like it was yesterday and thinking, *I don't really know what I want to do for a living right now, but I will encourage my classmates to go on to do great things.*

Being a close-knit class, Judy had taken a liking to another senior boy named Brad, and was his steady girlfriend for two years. Brad was a wheat farmer, so he had a steady income. Judy elected not to go to college and got married to Brad two years after they graduated from high school. They lived in a small house that his parents provided for them so he could help with the farming. After a year, Judy had her first baby boy and named him Taylor. She was content to stay home and take care of her little infant. Taylor grew into a toddler, and soon Judy and Brad had another baby boy and named him John. Judy stayed busy on the farm and took care of her two boys until they were ready to go to the Prairie Rose grade school. They did not have kindergarten there at the time, so Taylor entered first grade when he was six. He was eager to learn and did well in school.

A few years passed and it was time for John to go to first grade at Prairie Rose Grade School. Judy was sad because both of her boys were in school and she missed them. Lucky for her, the school superintendent approached her one day as she entered the school. He asked her, "Judy, I know you are very bright because I watched you grow up here in Prairie Rose, where you were an outstanding student. Our school secretary just retired and I need someone to take her place. Would you consider becoming our grade school secretary?"

Judy thought about it for a minute and said she would talk it over with her husband that night and get back to him the next day with her answer. Judy did discuss the possibility of working as the school secretary with her husband, and Brad thought it would be a good idea. He told her that she would be able to see her children every day and they would have the same holidays as she did. That was the selling point for her. She would also have the summers off so she could help with the farming. She told Brad she would give it a try.

Judy called the superintendent the next day and told him that she would like to take the job. Little did she know what she was getting into. Judy had to learn how to take attendance for the grade school every day and record it in her books. She also had to get the lunch count from each classroom in the morning so she could tell the school cooks how many people were eating that day. Sometimes when it was extremely cold outside, as it can be in North Dakota in the winter, Judy had to step into the cafeteria and watch the students play basketball, dodge ball, and other games because the wind chill was minus ten degrees and the students could not be outside. The teachers were eating their lunches and only had a half an hour before they went back to the classroom.

Since it was a small school with only fifty-six students from grades one to seniors in high school, the school did not have a school nurse and Judy was often asked to take a sick child out of the classroom and get him to lie down on a cot while she tried to reach his mother. More times than not, she also had to clean up after throw-up incidents and urinary accidents. It was all in a day's work for Judy, but she actually liked the fast pace of this job and did not have trouble keeping up. There were times that she thought she couldn't handle it all, but she greeted the parents with a large smile and knew she was doing something good to help the school. Judy stayed at that job for twenty years until she retired, and she said that if she had to do it over again, she would.

Author Bio: Judy lives in Prairie Rose with her husband, Brad. They have five grandchildren and enjoy taking them for hayrides in the winter. They also have a large sheep dog named Roxie who keeps them company all year long.

Terrific Teacher Aides: Can You Be My Grandma?

Jill Everson

Jill Everson grew up in Plentywood, Montana, with two siblings, Kelly and Randy. She was a cheerleader for the Plentywood Wildcats and after graduating from high school, she went to school at Rocky Mountain College for one year. She wanted to be a dental hygienist or an artist, but one of her parents discouraged her from doing that so she took classes in early childhood education instead.

She met Dwayne Everson, who was also from Plentywood, and eventually they were married. They had three boys: Taylor, Tanner, and Trent. Jill was content being a wife and mother and was an excellent homemaker.

After the boys graduated from Plentywood High School, Jill and Wayne moved to Billings, Montana. Jill applied for a position as a teacher's aide at a HeadStart program and she was hired to help with the three-to-five-year-old children.

One day she was called to the office of the director and she thought she had done something wrong. She sat across the desk from the director and was wondering what she was going to say. The director, Melissa Adams, said, "Jill, I just want you to know that I have never seen a person show as much empathy as you have for these little children."

Surprised at the comment, Jill asked, "Doesn't everyone who works here show the same amount of empathy?"

Melissa answered, "Sadly, no they don't. Thank you for the work you do here, Jill."

Jill left work that day floating on air.

She also remembers the day she was showing a little girl how to dish up her food for the lunch program. Her name was Julie, and when Jill was reaching over her to show her how to spoon out a dish, Julie touched her cheek and said, "You have such soft wrinkles. Can you be my grandma?"

Jill gave her a hug and thought, *this is why I do this job.* Jill worked at the HeadStart program for five years and enjoyed her time there hoping to enhance the lives of her students.

Author Bio: Jill lives in Billings with her husband Wayne and spends several months of the year in Arizona as 'snowbirds.' They love visiting their sons and they enjoy playing with their miniature schnauzer named Jax.

I Forgot to Raise My Hand

Amy Solberg

Amy Solberg didn't anticipate being a teacher's aide in the small town of Highmore, South Dakota. She had gone to school in Billings to be a cosmetologist. Being married to Mike Solberg, a rancher, was an exciting life where she was a homemaker and raised their three daughters: Paige, Shan, and Sierra. After three years, Amy and Mike had another baby who was born with cerebral palsy. His name was Hunter and everyone in the family adored him. It was difficult at times because Hunter suffered from epilepsy as well, so he had debilitating seizures many times throughout the year.

When it came time for Hunter to attend kindergarten at Highmore Elementary School, the superintendent approached Amy and asked her if she would consider being a teacher's aide for Hunter. Who would know him better than his mother? Amy thought about it and decided this would be a good idea.

She was a little worried about how the other students would accept Hunter in the classroom, since he sometimes made noises and did odd things. He couldn't talk or walk at the time, so it seemed like it might be helpful to guide him through the day. She would also be close to give him medications if he had a seizure.

The first day was a little rough, but that night the teacher called the parents of the other students and explained about Hunter's situation. The next day, the students came up to Hunter and wanted to play with him and be with him. Amy felt much better so she settled into the routine of the classroom and listened to Mrs. Clancy teach her lessons.

One day, Mrs. Clancy was teaching the kindergartners about the different kinds of fruits. She asked the students which fruit had seeds on the outside, and Amy burst out, "Strawberries!"

One of the students turned back and looked at her and said, "Amy, we were supposed to answer that question."

Another day, Mrs. Clancy told the students that if you kept apples in a cellar they could last up to two years. Amy had never heard that fact before and she called out, "Are you kidding me?"

Again the students gave her the evil eye and one of them said rather indignantly, "Amy, you are supposed to raise your hand."

Amy had forgotten the rules but the students and Mrs. Clancy soon forgave her.

The students all accepted Hunter and would fight over taking turns to push him in his wheelchair and spend time with him. She continued her work at the school for three years. Then she felt that Hunter and the teachers knew what to do in difficult situations and decided to return home to care for her family. She had a new baby girl named Savannah and wanted to stay home and take care of her.

It was good for the students to have Hunter in the classroom. Amy's last day of being Hunter's teacher's aide ended on a poignant note. As she walked out the door one of the little girls grabbed her hand and said, "Amy, you are so lucky."

Amy responded, "Why is that honey?"

The little girl answered, "Because you get to be with Hunter all the time."

Author Bio: Amy lives with her husband Mike in Highmore, South Dakota. They farm and operate The Grand Lodge, where they take guests pheasant hunting. Amy is the head cook for the lodge and she is pleased that all her grown children still live in Highmore. Amy and Mike have eight grandchildren and love sharing the holidays with them.

CONCLUSION
The Endeth Cometh

After sharing true stories from some of our unsung heroes in the schoolyard, I have some new thoughts for you. There are certain things we can do to stop the 'pig on the playground' from causing chaos in our school system.

For example, to address the teacher shortage, some school districts in the United States offer to pay the schooling costs for someone to become a certified teacher. If they take this offer, they have to commit to teaching in that school district for three years.

Housing is so expensive these days, so some school districts arrange to buy a home for an incoming teacher as a bonus for signing on in their district.

Many universities in the United States have a fast track for certifying teachers who already have a bachelor's degree in some area and want to teach that subject matter. These programs are called the Master's in Teaching Program and they only take one year to complete.

To address the shortage of school bus drivers, school districts should have bus fairs and allow ordinary citizens to see what it takes to be a bus driver. They should also give bonuses to bus drivers who stay in the district year after year.

We, as ordinary citizens need to write to our state congressmen and women and ask them to become aware of the problems we are having retaining teachers. We must ask them to give our teachers a salary that is commensurate with other professionals that are in the real world. After all, how would we have doctors, lawyers, nurses, CEOs, computer programmers, electricians, plumbers, and other professions if we didn't learn how to read, write, do math, and acquire other skills from a teacher?

If we all work together to improve the state of education, we can catch that pig!

Acknowledgments

I would like to thank Cristina Smith, Lynn Tramonte, Valerie Costa, Christy Day and Collett Gilmore for helping me bring this book to fruition.

I would also like to thank my first readers, Fauna Allen and Debbie Stein Savino for their helpful suggestions regarding the content of the book.

Special thanks to my daughter, Kathleen Treichel for the wonderful illustrations. My granddaughters, Chloe Brooke Gilmore and Selah Pearl Young also contributed their talents for the illustrations.

Thank you to all the teachers, teacher aides, maintenance men, coaches, principals, education professors, homeschool teachers, school cooks, school secretaries, librarians and bus drivers for sharing your lives with us. You are our unsung heroes.

Finally, I would like to thank Dr. Paul Gathercoal, former chair of the department of Curriculum and Instruction at the University of Idaho, because he believed in me.

In writing this book I hope to inspire others to join in the noble profession of teaching and other jobs that are required to educate the children of America.

About the Author

Deanna and her husband, Rick, taught in Alaska in remote Inupiat and Yupik villages for eight years. She defines this experience as pivotal in understanding the value of other cultures. Upon returning to the 'lower forty-eight,' Deanna taught Native Americans at Paschal Sherman Indian School in Omak, Washington.

At the age of fifty-nine, Deanna returned to Washington State University (WSU), where she received her Ph.D. in Literacy. After teaching courses at WSU and presenting at conferences across the United States and in Japan, she transferred to the University of Idaho, where she was a lecturer and an affiliate assistant professor for pre-service teachers in the Department of Curriculum and Instruction. In 2010, the Gamma Phi Beta women's sorority at the University of Idaho selected her as the Outstanding Professor of the Year. In addition, Dr. Gilmore received the University of Idaho Alumni Award for Excellence for her contribution to the academic development of her students.

Dr. Gilmore is now retired and enjoys contacting her former students through Facebook and Instagram posts. Her husband thinks she spends too much time on her phone.